# Praise for *The Grail Code*

"*The Grail Code* is a lucid treatment of the Grail legends, based on real history. **It satisfies the hunger that people have for knowledge of this mystery. The true Grail bears witness to a divine gift that exceeds even the deepest human longing.** This book is unique and a great read."
—SCOTT HAHN, author of *The Lamb's Supper* and
*Hail, Holy Queen*

"In Western literature, the search for the Holy Grail is a recurring and engaging theme. In whatever form it takes, the spiritual overtones are compelling. While many authors have addressed the quest, Mike Aquilina and Christopher Bailey bring a fresh approach. *The Grail Code: Quest for the Real Presence* **is both a good read and an invitation to experience a sense of spiritual journey holding the reader's imagination in the context of faith.**"
—MOST REVEREND DONALD W. WUERL, STD,
bishop of Pittsburgh

"*The Grail Code: Quest for the Real Presence* is a much-needed book, immersing the reader in the richness of Grail lore through the ages. **The book grounds the legends in their historical and theological context, giving a much-needed corrective to some of the more outlandish and unfortunately popular constructs of the legend we find today.**"
—AMY WELBORN, author of *De-coding Da Vinci*

"**What is the *real* meaning of the Holy Grail? Aquilina and Bailey supply the answer in a dazzling mix of scholarship and spiritual insight packaged in highly readable prose.** *The Grail Code* is a learning experience and also a treat."
—RUSSELL SHAW, writer and journalist

"Aquilina and Bailey in *The Grail Code: Quest for the Real Presence* have uncovered the reasons behind the fascination—past and present—over the Holy Grail and its quest. They have accomplished this by doing some real research and finding real *facts* about the Grail literature of old, unlike some contemporary writers in their more popular books. And more importantly, **they have identified the religious significance of this search, for the Christian.** A great read for any Grail enthusiast!"
—REV. T. G. MORROW, STD, author of
*Christian Courtship in an Oversexed World*

"What is it about the Holy Grail that's so beautiful and compelling as to inspire knights, kings, and millions of readers for almost a thousand years? **This is the only book that answers the question. Read it and begin your quest.**"

—DAVID SCOTT, author of *The Catholic Passion*

"This is a compelling meditation on the legend of the Holy Grail and its interplay with Christian spirituality. **The book draws on centuries of beliefs about Holy Communion, the history of European literature and changing cultural ideas of love and sin to illuminate why the Grail legend became so popular, and how it changed through time.** Despite its intellectual sweep, the book is written in an engaging style for the casual reader. This should be a helpful reference for anyone who has been intrigued by *The Da Vinci Code*."

—ANN RODGERS, religion reporter for *The Pittsburgh Post-Gazette*

"*The Grail Code: Quest for the Real Presence* will tell you, if you let it, what the Narnia stories of C. S. Lewis really are about and why they remain so popular. The genius of the book is this: It dares reveal that the secret of medieval romance is to be found where it is least expected—in plain sight. The authors—learned amateurs in the best sense—have avoided both academic jargon and commercial hype so that contemporary readers may discover, as did the heroes of the old Romantic stories, **that the blessing of redemption that they sought in strange and distant lands is to be found in humble, ordinary places, everywhere the sacraments of Penance and the Eucharist are celebrated.** This is a book that faithful readers of all ages will be enriched by."

—FRANK T. ZBOZNY, professor of medieval English literature, Duquesne University

"Aquilina and Bailey have produced the indispensable layman's compendium of all things concerning the Holy Grail. Leave it to clever and disciplined journalists to do what ecclesiastical historians and biblical archaeologists had not: connect the arcane and intractable passage of the Holy Grail to the literary and cultural drama that has gripped our civilization and every soul in it for centuries. *The Da Vinci Code* is destined for ultimate deconstruction, but *The Grail Code: Quest for the Real Presence* **will undoubtedly long serve seekers on the ageless quest for the vessel of divine blessing** or the pathway back to ancient Camelot."

—MARK GRUBER, OSB, professor of anthropology, St. Vincent College

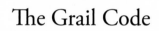

The Grail Code

# The Grail CODE

## Quest for the Real Presence

Mike Aquilina and Christopher Bailey

LoyolaPress.

Chicago

# LOYOLAPRESS.

3441 N. ASHLAND AVENUE
CHICAGO, ILLINOIS 60657
(800) 621-1008
WWW.LOYOLABOOKS.ORG

*Cover design by Adam Moroschan*
*Interior design by Kathryn Seckman Kirsch*

**Library of Congress Cataloging-in-Publication Data**
Aquilina, Mike.
  The Grail code : quest for the real presence / Mike Aquilina and Christopher Bailey.
    p. cm.
  Includes bibliographical references and index.
  ISBN-13: 978-0-8294-2159-0 (alk. paper)
  ISBN-10: 0-8294-2159-9 (alk. paper)
    1. Spiritual life—Catholic Church. 2. Last Supper. 3. Lord's Supper. 4. Grail. I. Bailey, Christopher, 1964– II. Title.
BX2350.3.A65 2006
001.94—dc22

2006001611

Printed in the United States of America
06 07 08 09 10 11 12 Versa 10 9 8 7 6 5 4 3 2 1

To Rosemary and Simon

# Contents

✝

# Preface

## The Ancient Mystery and the Real Presence

Are we worthy to achieve the Grail? Are we ready to walk with God in paradise?

Even today, millions of people thirst for the Holy Grail. We see the image of it everywhere, in our favorite books and movies. It's a symbol of everything that's mysterious and desirable. And at its heart is the greatest mystery of all: the mystery of the Eucharist—of God with us, of Christ's real presence—body, blood, soul, and divinity.

But too often we lose our way when we begin the historical phase of our quest for the Grail. We end up mired in a slough of faux conspiracy theories, or we chase ever wispier sprites of Celtic mythology. Carelessly we empty the Grail of its precious blood, and when that happens we lose the Grail itself.

The real story of the Holy Grail is a true adventure, with plenty of surprising twists and unexpected discoveries. It's a long journey through the back streets of history, from the Palestine of Jesus Christ to Britain in the shadow of the Dark Ages, from the colorful courts of medieval France to the grim insanity of Hitler's Germany. And the prize waiting for us at the end of our adventure is nothing less than a communion with Jesus Christ himself.

That's what makes the journey worthwhile. When we see it through the lens of the Grail stories, we realize that the Christian life itself is a perilous but glorious adventure. The Grail legends touch something deep in the human heart, something that was placed there by the God who created the world and redeemed it, and who gave the world his only Son. That's the real mystery of the Grail, and that's the beginning of our quest.

And so we begin.

✝

# Chapter the First

## In Which Our Enterprise Begins with a Question and an Answer

THIS IS A BOOK ABOUT LONGING and desire—our longing for the unattainable, and our burning desire to attain it anyway.

Human longing is older than history, and it drives history. It is part of our very creation, a hole in our hearts so big that nothing can fill it. Like a spiritual DNA, it goes with being human. It may be quieted for a time. It may be damped down for a time. But the code is there, driving us on to seek whatever might fill that hole.

When we do find something that seems for a moment to fill that interior chasm, one phrase springs instantly to our lips: we have found the Holy Grail.

### The Insatiable Longing

What is at the root of our undying desire? Why do thrill seekers jump out of airplanes? Why do tyrants destroy their countries in a single-minded pursuit of power? Why do firefighters rush into burning buildings even when the rescue seems hopeless? Why do suicide bombers blow themselves to bits in the name of their country or their religion? Why do martyrs die with hymns on their lips?

Isn't it because they sense, at almost a preconscious level, that the ordinary things of this world—living and eating and sleeping—just aren't enough?

The gods of the Canaanites, the Aztecs, and any number of other refined and sophisticated cultures demanded human sacrifice. Sometimes worshipers sacrificed their own children. Why? Were they just superstitious savages? Or were they looking for the right thing in the wrong way?

We, too, try to fulfill our deepest self in ways that satisfy us temporarily—with glory, money, thrills, sex. But our emptiness is infinitely bigger than our feverish activities and conquests.

The Buddhists say that earthly desires lead to enlightenment. They don't mean, of course, that the way to reach enlightenment is by indulging every whim. They mean that our earthly desires point the way to what we're really longing for. Our desire for power, wealth, sex, shiny cars, or whatever it is we think we really want is only an expression of the true hunger we are unable to name.

Christians have a similar saying: grace builds on nature. That deep and insatiable longing we all feel is implanted in us at creation. And although it can drive us to all kinds of sins, God will use it to pull us closer—if we consent.

That longing and that grace are really what the stories of the Holy Grail are about.

## The Story of the Grail

The story of the quest for the Holy Grail has dominated the English-speaking world like no other myth or legend. Its elements even predate the English language. Poets, novelists, and filmmakers have told the story of the quest again and again: it doesn't get old or tiresome or go out of style. The adventure of the pilgrimage is what everyone wants, but not nearly so much as the goal.

These days, most people know the Holy Grail from books like *The Da Vinci Code* and *Holy Blood, Holy Grail,* or from Monty Python. What we've lost in these pop culture transformations of the Grail is what made it holy in the first place. That original meaning is what this book seeks to unfold.

In popular entertainment we see all kinds of attempts at understanding the Grail.

The movie *Excalibur* tried very hard to give us a pagan grail. The secret that led to the Grail was simply this: "The king and the land are one." The movie's interpretation did give us one of cinema's rivetingly beautiful moments: Arthur and his knights, roused from their lethargy, ride forth to their last battle, and the wasteland turns green and fertile in their path. But does anyone in our age of republics and constitutional monarchies actually *believe* that the king and the land are one? We have a hard enough time believing that we actually elected our congresses and parliaments. The message has nothing in it for us: it leaves us unsatisfied and wishing for something deeper.

*The Da Vinci Code,* by Dan Brown, gave us a reinter-pretation of the Grail—as a holy bloodline, the lineage of Jesus Christ and his supposed wife, Mary Magdalene. It was already a popular idea long before the novel came out: Michael Baigent, Richard Leigh, and Henry Lincoln's book *Holy Blood, Holy Grail* had been a best seller for twenty years, and Dan Brown took his Grail ideas from there. The reinterpretation gives us the lure of a deeply hidden secret that is centuries old, and the promise of enlightenment once we know the secret. That so many people have been enchanted with the notion proves it has some attractive power; the main problem with it is that the historical foundations of such a hypothesis are easily dismantled.

Other modern Grail stories have dwelled on the swash-buckling adventure of the quest but remained deliberately fuzzy about the nature of the Grail itself. *Indiana Jones and the Last Crusade* gave us a Grail that seemed to have something to do with Christian legend and that—like the Grail in the best medieval romances—rewarded the worthy and punished the unworthy. "But choose wisely," says the ancient knight who guards the Grail and dozens of decoy grails, "for as the true Grail will bring you life, the false grail will take it from you." And soon enough, expensive special effects show us exactly what the knight means.

But Hollywood could not confront the whole force of the Christian symbolism in the Grail legends: we're never quite sure what the Grail really means for Indiana Jones, and it's just as well that the quest is entertaining enough to distract us from asking too many questions about the object of it. Asked what he found in the Grail, Indiana Jones's father, Henry, says, "Illumination"—which really could mean anything. Practically speaking, neither he nor his son seems very much changed by meeting the Grail. And that's a bit surprising when we consider that the whole purpose of seeking the Grail is usually to change the seeker's life. If nothing is changed, then the longing is still there, unfulfilled.

Revived pagan mythology, anti-Christian propaganda, swashbuckling adventure—none of these give an adequate account of why the Grail legend has survived. After all, the empty Grail is just a cup.

# Chapter the Second

## Which Reveals the True Origin
## of the Holy Cup

Are you able to drink the cup that I am about to drink?"

This is the question that begins our quest for the Holy Grail. Every seeker of the Grail must answer it: can I drink from the Grail?

Yet it seemed like such an odd question when it was first asked. Two of Jesus' disciples, James and John—the "Sons of Thunder," as he liked to call them—had asked him a favor. Or rather, as Matthew remembered it, their mother had asked it for them: "Declare that these two sons of mine will sit, one at your right hand and one at your left, in your kingdom."

James and John had been with Jesus for a long time already, and still they didn't seem to know what they were looking for. They wanted *something* desperately enough that they were willing to give up everything and follow an itinerant preacher who always had to keep one step ahead of the authorities. They seemed to think their longing could be fulfilled by some position of power and honor in an earthly kingdom.

Instead of simply telling their mother that her wish was granted, or telling her to stop asking for ridiculous favors, Jesus grew suddenly solemn. He turned to James and John and addressed them directly.

"You do not know what you are asking," he told them. "Are you able to drink the cup that I am about to drink?"

They probably didn't understand the question. They may have been thinking of a royal banquet, and a little wine never hurt anybody. So they immediately answered, "We are able."

We'll see the same thoughtless enthusiasm at the beginning of every Grail quest. Our longing is so deep and desperate that it blinds us to the consequences of what we undertake.

Jesus answered, "You will indeed drink my cup, but to sit at my right hand and at my left, this is not mine to grant, but it is for those for whom it has been prepared by my Father" (Matthew 20:20–23).

What an unsatisfying answer! It must have left them entirely baffled. The only thing they could possibly understand was that they were not being promised the posts of first and second minister in Jesus' coming kingdom.

Still, at least they would drink from Jesus' cup. They would have some important place in the kingdom, some position elevated above the common herd. Would that be enough to satisfy them?

During the next few days, James and John must have thought quite a bit about their positions in the coming kingdom. Jesus entered Jerusalem in triumph, with cheering crowds carpeting his path with palm fronds and their own clothes, shouting, "Blessed is the king / who comes in the name of the Lord!" (Luke 19:38). It must have seemed as though Jesus' glorious kingdom was just around the corner.

## Blood of the New Covenant

It quickly became clear that the coming of Jesus' kingdom wasn't going to be easy. The ruling powers were set against Jesus—even to the point that Jesus and his disciples had to make their Passover preparations in secret. At that Passover meal, Jesus seemed in an unusually somber mood. He told his disciples that one of them would betray him, which they could hardly believe.

> While they were eating, he took a loaf of bread, and after blessing it he broke it, gave it to them, and said, "Take; this is my body." Then he took a cup, and after giving thanks he gave it to them, and all of them drank from it. He said to them, "This is my blood of the covenant, which is poured out for many." (Mark 14:22–24)

"This is my blood of the covenant." It takes some imagination to hear those words the way the disciples originally heard them. We hear them every Sunday; the disciples heard them for the first time at the Last Supper, and they must have been both shocked and confused.

They recognized the allusion, of course. Centuries before, at Sinai, Moses gave the people of Israel the law that God had given him. Then he built an altar and sacrificed oxen on it. Half the blood he sprinkled on the altar; the other half he sprinkled on the people, binding them in a ritual covenant with God. "See the blood of the covenant that the LORD has made with you in accordance with all these words," Moses announced (Exodus 24:8).

Blood was a powerful thing in the Scriptures: "For the life of the flesh is in the blood; and I have given it to you for making atonement for your lives on the altar; for, as life, it is the blood that makes atonement" (Leviticus 17:11).

We can imagine how the disciples' minds must have reeled when Jesus introduced these familiar words with a twist: "Blood of the covenant" could only mean something like the covenant ratified at Sinai, the covenant that was the basis of every aspect of Jewish life. And Jesus said it was his own blood. He was putting himself in the place of the sacrifice, giving them his own blood to make atonement for their souls.

And was he really asking them to drink it? That very passage from the law about blood making atonement went on to say, "Therefore I have said to the people of Israel:

No person among you shall eat blood, nor shall any alien who resides among you eat blood" (Leviticus 17:12). The law against partaking of blood was so fundamental to the order of the cosmos that even the Gentiles were supposed to obey it.

It must have been almost too much for the disciples to take in. What were they thinking as the cup made its way around the table? Did some of them shiver as the cup approached them? Did some of them hesitate before drinking?

Could they drink the cup that Jesus was going to drink?

"Truly I tell you," Jesus said as the cup was making its rounds, "I will never again drink of the fruit of the vine until that day when I drink it new in the kingdom of God" (Mark 14:25). What did he mean by that?

And, as many readers over the centuries have wondered as they read the accounts of the Last Supper, what sort of cup was this that Jesus passed around?

## The Secrets of the Cup

We can translate the Greek word for "cup" a number of ways. We can call the vessel a cup, a chalice, a bowl—even a grail, which originally comes from a Latin word for a shallow dish.

Jesus and his disciples were poor, so we might at first suppose that whatever cup they used was simple and cheap. On the other hand, they had borrowed a furnished dining room for the occasion. "Go into the city," Jesus had told two of his disciples, "and a man carrying a jar of water will meet you; follow him, and wherever he enters, say to the owner of the house, 'The Teacher asks, Where is my guest room where I may eat the Passover with my disciples?' He will show you a large room upstairs, furnished and ready. Make preparations for us there" (Mark 14:13–15).

It all sounds a bit cloak-and-dagger: go into the city and look for the man with the jug; follow him (but don't say anything) until he enters a house; then say the secret password, and someone will let you in. But this secrecy is hardly surprising: Jesus knew he was in imminent danger of arrest, and anyone who gave him aid and comfort might be in just as much trouble. This householder might have been one of the many well-to-do followers of Jesus—someone especially vulnerable to punishment by the authorities if it became known that he associated with the Teacher.

At least he was well-to-do enough to provide a furnished dining room. As such, it likely came with a cup suitable for an important ceremony like a Passover meal.

Ordinary drinking cups of the time were usually made of earthenware. But a ceremonial cup would probably be made of something more valuable: bronze, perhaps, or silver, or glass, or even gold, if the owner was rich enough. Many early Christian chalices were made of glass. Were the early Christians keeping alive the memory of the actual cup Jesus used? Or was glass just the most dignified thing they could get if the congregation couldn't afford a gold chalice?

So the actual cup could have been almost anything. It could have been an ordinary drinking cup, or it could have been something quite expensive and ornate.

After the cup was passed, Jesus and his disciples sang a hymn. Jesus had many things to say to them, some of which they didn't really understand. And there was an awkward little scene with Judas Iscariot, the treasurer of the group. "Do quickly what you are going to do," Jesus said to Judas, and without a word, Judas got up and walked out into the night (John 13:27–30). What was that all about?

Then the group went out to the Mount of Olives. Almost certainly they left the room to be cleaned up later, either by themselves or by their host's servants.

In a garden nearby, Jesus went a little way away from his disciples and prayed, "Father, if you are willing, remove this cup from me; yet, not my will but yours be done."

It was a prayer of anguish; the "cup" he was about to drink would be a cup of unbearable suffering. "In his anguish he prayed more earnestly, and his sweat became like great drops of blood falling down on the ground" (Luke 22:42, 44).

And suddenly Jesus was arrested by a squadron of Roman soldiers—with Judas Iscariot leading them—and the disciples scattered like sheep with no shepherd.

Sometime that night or the next day—while Jesus was being beaten and tortured, or while he was dying in agony on the cross—the dishes were cleaned up and put away.

✝

# Chapter the Third

## In Which We Seek the Holy Cup
## and Find the Eucharist

LONG AFTER THE CRUCIFIXION AND THE Resurrection, Jesus' most devoted followers continued to meet in the upper room. In fact, it became the first Christian church. The house itself was one of the few buildings to survive the destruction of Jerusalem in AD 70: St. Epiphanius, who wrote in the 300s, tells us that when Christians staggered back to the burned and ruined city, they found the place still standing and went back to their old habit of meeting there.

The owner of the house must also have been an enthusiastic Christian; otherwise he wouldn't have risked so much to give Jesus and his disciples a place to meet. If the cup was part of the household furnishings, then it probably stayed with the house, and it belonged to a Christian.

## Revealed in the Breaking of the Bread

It is quite likely that the Christians continued to use the cup when they repeated the ceremony that Jesus taught them at the Last Supper. This was the central ceremony of the Way, as they called their new faith. At this point, they had no other name for their practice. They didn't think of it as a new religion; they thought of it as a better understanding of their religion—an understanding that included the wonderful knowledge that they were living in the age of the Messiah.

The Eucharist—a Greek word that means "thanksgiving"—was at the heart of their practice right from the beginning. "They devoted themselves to the apostles' teaching and fellowship, to the breaking of bread and the prayers" (Acts 2:42). We notice right away that "the breaking of bread" comes first, before "the prayers."

Luke illustrates what the breaking of bread meant to Jesus' followers with a story of something that happened the day Jesus rose from the dead. Two of Jesus' followers were walking along the road to Emmaus, a little village some distance outside Jerusalem. They had heard the strange story of the empty tomb, but they didn't know what to make of it. While they were walking and talking gloomily about the death of their Teacher, they met a stranger who asked them what they were talking about.

"Are you the only stranger in Jerusalem who does not know the things that have taken place there in these days?" asked one of them.

"What things?" the stranger asked.

"The things about Jesus of Nazareth," they answered. We can imagine them both talking at once, telling the ignorant stranger who the famous Jesus was, how they had expected him to be the Messiah, but how instead he had died in disgrace. They even told him the strange story of the empty tomb.

"Oh, how foolish you are," the stranger said when they had finished their story, "and how slow of heart to believe all that the prophets have declared! Was it not necessary that the Messiah should suffer these things and then enter into his glory?" And, much to their surprise, he interpreted the story they had just told him in the light of Moses and the prophets, showing them how everything had been foretold.

When they reached Emmaus, it was already late, so they invited the stranger to stay with them for dinner. While he was eating with them, he took bread, said the blessing, broke the bread, and gave it to them. Then suddenly they knew who the stranger was. It was Jesus himself! They recognized him in the breaking of the bread. But as soon as they recognized him, he was gone. Or, rather, he was still there, but in a different way: they were left with the bread he had given them (Luke 24:13–35).

## Salvation or Judgment

The first Christians had a powerful sense that Jesus was really present in the Eucharist—that the bread and wine really were his body and blood. The cup was a cup of salvation: it was the Savior really coming to them.

> What shall I return to the LORD
>> for all his bounty to me?
> I will lift up the cup of salvation
>> and call on the name of the LORD . . .
> I will offer to you a thanksgiving sacrifice
>> and call on the name of the LORD.
>> (Psalm 116:12–13, 17)

This psalm is used in Christian liturgies all over the world, and Christians everywhere recognize the Eucharist in the "cup of salvation" and "thanksgiving sacrifice."

But the cup of salvation can also be a cup of judgment.

> Whoever, therefore, eats the bread or drinks the cup of the Lord in an unworthy manner will be answerable for the body and blood of the Lord. Examine yourselves, and only then eat of the bread and drink of the cup. For all who eat and drink without discerning the body, eat and drink judgment against themselves.
> (1 Corinthians 11:27–29)

It is not a light or easy thing to take the cup of salvation. On the contrary, only the worthy may drink from the

Grail. Paul is not exaggerating here; he believes this is literally a matter of life and death. "For this reason many of you are weak and ill," he continues, "and some have died" (1 Corinthians 11:30).

For the worthy, who discern the Lord's body in the Eucharist, it is the communion of the body and blood of Jesus Christ. For the unworthy, it is judgment. That's the way the Holy Grail works.

Nor is it always easy even for the worthy to drink the cup. "Are you able to drink the cup that I am about to drink?" The cup that Jesus drank was crucifixion and death. Many of his most beloved followers would have to drink the same cup.

But suffering was not a thing Christians dreaded the way other people did. It could be a joyous sacrifice. In fact, the early Christians often spoke of their own sufferings in language that makes it clear they were thinking of the sacrifice of the Eucharist.

"I am already being poured out as a libation, and the time of my departure has come," Paul wrote to his friend Timothy (2 Timothy 4:6). Paul was in prison in Rome, waiting for the time when he, too, would drink the cup that Jesus drank. Nevertheless, he did not resent his suffering. Like other Christians facing martyrdom, he remembered what Jesus had said: "Do not fear those who kill the body but cannot kill the soul; rather fear him who can destroy both soul and body in hell" (Matthew 10:28).

## "We Cannot Live without the Mass"

In all the best Grail stories, and in all the best Christian art, the Holy Grail is a Eucharistic image. Even pop culture (think of Indiana Jones) presents it to us as the cup of the Last Supper. The Grail stands for the central mystery of the Christian liturgy, and for the central promise of the Christian faith—the promise that our longing to meet God has a fulfillment.

The central importance of the Eucharist was something Christians assumed. "We cannot live without the Mass," one North African martyr told his persecutors in the reign of Diocletian, a notorious murderer of Christians.

That leads us back to the question of what happened to the cup Jesus used at the Last Supper.

An early Christian might have answered that what happened to it doesn't matter at all. Every consecrated chalice was the Holy Grail, containing the true blood of the Lord. And every chalice was treated that way. Even when Christianity was a capital offense and most of its followers were poor, the Christians scraped together enough money to buy expensive fittings for their underground churches. When police raided one house-church, they confiscated quite a list of treasures, which were duly recorded by the court:

- 2 golden chalices
- 6 silver chalices

- 6 silver dishes
- 1 silver bowl
- 7 silver lamps
- 7 short bronze lamp stands, with lamps
- 11 bronze lamps on chains[1]

This was not extravagance. It was the only way these poor people knew of expressing their reverence for the Eucharist, which they literally valued more than their own lives.

About a century later, in St. Jerome's time, the bishop of Toulouse sold off his church's gold and silver to feed the poor. He had to use a wooden basket and a glass chalice to hold the Eucharist. Jerome defended him: "What can be more rich than the man who carries the body of Christ in a basket of wickerwork and the blood of Christ in a vessel of glass?"[2]

Jerome's defense tells us that by his time, glass chalices were rare. A larger church, at least, was expected to have a golden chalice; there must have been quite a bit of grumbling in Toulouse when the bishop introduced a glass chalice. The reason is obvious: the people revered the blood of Christ so greatly that a glass chalice seemed almost blasphemously common. Jerome had to remind them that it was the blood that made the chalice precious, not the other way round.

As stoutly as Jerome defended the bishop of Toulouse and his cheap glass chalice, he also demanded a high standard of reverence for the Eucharistic vessels, no matter what they were made of. It was necessary, he wrote, to make the people understand "that the sacred chalices, veils, and other accessories used in the celebration of the Lord's passion are not mere lifeless and senseless objects devoid of holiness, but that rather, from their association with the body and blood of the Lord, they are to be venerated with the same awe as the Body and Blood themselves." [3]

Although the Eucharist was the holiest treasure, the vessels that carried it, by their office, were also holy treasures that demanded reverence. So we can easily imagine that some of the early Christians might have particularly treasured the cup that Jesus had used. Not only was it a vessel for the Eucharist, but it was also a rare memento of Jesus, who in his life had never accumulated much property.

## But What Happened to the Cup?

If these early Christians maintained possession of the cup, they would have taken care to protect it when danger threatened, carrying it with them when they fled the city as the Roman legions relentlessly approached. Later, as the church grew more prosperous, the Holy Grail, as we might call the cup, would have been ever more precious as a relic of the earthly ministry of the Lord Jesus Christ.

Today, when we have something we think of as an antique, we try to preserve it in as close to its original condition as possible. But in ancient times, and on through the Middle Ages, the common way of showing veneration for a precious relic was to surround it with rich ornamentation. Thus the Christians, as soon as they had the money and the freedom, built splendid churches on all the sites associated with the earthly life of Christ. Bits of bone from famous martyrs—infinitely more precious than diamonds to the Christians—were set like gems in elaborate fittings of gold. A relic might even accumulate multiple layers of ornamentation, as successive generations of donors expressed their veneration for the holy object.

If there was a real Holy Grail—a cup venerated by the early Christians as the cup used at the Last Supper—then it would eventually have become so encrusted with jewels and precious metals from the far corners of the earth that the original object would be hard to recognize. The cup would have been unchanged in essence but surrounded by a superstructure of ornamentation designed to draw attention to the beauty of its holiness.[4]

All this is simply speculation. In spite of the strong claims about some relics in various parts of Europe, we really have no idea what became of the cup that Jesus used. Whether or not the object still exists, the veneration and ornamentation that might have happened to the Holy Grail is exactly what did happen to the *story* of the Holy Grail. One generation after another added jewels from all kinds of unlikely sources until the thing seemed to have a completely different shape. But the essence—the original meaning of the Eucharist—was unchanged. The added layers of ornament only expressed centuries of veneration for the truth of the Eucharist.

And all the legends begin with one real historical character: Joseph of Arimathea.

+

# Chapter the Fourth

Which Introduces the Paragon of Christian
Knighthood, Joseph of Arimathea

O F ALL THE CHARACTERS IN THE Gospel
accounts, the one most important in the Holy
Grail stories (besides Jesus Christ, of course) is
one most Christians hardly think about today.

Still, though the Gospels have little to say about him,
Joseph of Arimathea must have been a singularly coura-
geous man. The Gospels tell his story in spare and simple
terms, but his life—at least the years when he knew
Jesus—must have been one of high drama.

## A Friend on the Council

Joseph, the custodian of the Grail in the romances that
developed during the medieval period, appears in all four
Gospels. He was a follower of Jesus, though he kept it secret
for fear of Jesus' enemies, and he was also a member of the
Sanhedrin, or "council"—the Jewish governing body that

condemned Jesus for blasphemy and handed him over to be crucified. Joseph "had not agreed to their plan and action" (Luke 23:50). He was not the only member of the council who was also a follower of Jesus; we can imagine how lively Jesus' trial must have been. Or perhaps the highly irregular, and probably illegal, midnight trial of Jesus was arranged in that way to keep his friends on the council from finding out about it until it was too late.

For whatever reason, Joseph had not been able to prevent the Crucifixion, but he was determined to make up for it in the only way he could think of.

> When evening had come, and since it was the day of Preparation, that is, the day before the sabbath, Joseph of Arimathea, a respected member of the council, who was also himself waiting expectantly for the kingdom of God, went boldly to Pilate and asked for the body of Jesus. Then Pilate wondered if he were already dead; and summoning the centurion, he asked him whether he had been dead for some time. When he learned from the centurion that he was dead, he granted the body to Joseph. Then Joseph bought a linen cloth, and taking down the body, wrapped it in the linen cloth, and laid it in a tomb that had been hewn out of the rock. He then rolled a stone against the door of the tomb. (Mark 15:42–46)

That's about as much as we know about Joseph of Arimathea from Scripture. But he turned into one of the most romantic and adventurous figures in pious legend. When Jesus had already died on the cross, as John tells us, "one of the soldiers pierced his side with a spear, and at once blood and water came out" (John 19:34). In the legends, it was Joseph of Arimathea who stood at the foot of the cross and caught the blood and water that flowed from his side. And the vessel in which he caught it was that same cup Jesus had used at the Last Supper. Joseph became the custodian of the Holy Grail: the original cup of the Eucharist, literally filled with the true blood of the Savior.

## The Grail Moves to Britain

About thirty years afterward, the legends tell us, Joseph left Jerusalem with Philip the apostle to spread the gospel in Gaul, the Roman province that roughly corresponds to present-day France. When they had preached their way right through Gaul, Philip sent Joseph across the Channel to preach in Britain.

This is only legend, of course, and there is not a scrap of evidence to suggest it is anything more, other than old traditions in the part of Britain where Joseph was supposed to have settled. But the legend itself is not implausible. By the time the legends claim Joseph got there, Britain had been conquered and pacified by the Romans. It was now just another province in the same big Roman Empire that

ruled Jerusalem and the whole Mediterranean. A trip to
Britain would have been a long one, but there would have
been no special difficulties along the way. The overland
route through Gaul was safe and civilized; the Channel
crossing was a bit choppy but otherwise not much of an
adventure. There were no borders to cross, no passports
to stamp, no customs officials to bribe. Furthermore, we
have some good evidence that pockets of Christianity
had already appeared in Britain even before the Roman
conquest. We have no way of judging whether the legend
of Joseph has any basis in fact, but it was an easy legend
to believe.

At any rate, it matters very little to us whether the
legends about Joseph of Arimathea are true, because they
teach us a deeper and more important truth. They show
us how central the Eucharist was in medieval Christianity.
Jesus must have handled many thousands of objects during
his life on earth, but the cup of the Last Supper was the one
around which all the colorful legends grew. Only the true
cross fascinated Christian relic collectors and tale spinners
as much. For medieval Christians, the Last Supper was
the central event of Jesus' ministry, and all the stories spun
around the holy cup only confirm how holy the Eucharist
was to the people who heard those stories.

We've followed Joseph to Britain, and there (the stories
say) he settled down with the Holy Grail. He built a tiny
church at Glastonbury; well into the High Middle Ages,
the monks of the abbey that was established there showed

pilgrims a small wattle-and-daub chapel and claimed that it was Joseph's.

With Joseph, then, the story of the Holy Grail moves to Britain and Glastonbury. Now, Glastonbury is remarkable for another famous association: local legend insists that Glastonbury was Avalon, King Arthur's final resting place.

From here on, the story of the Holy Grail is inextricably entwined with the story of King Arthur—a story of creation, fall, and longed-for redemption.

✝

# Chapter the Fifth

---

## In Which We Seek the King Arthur of History and Find Instead a Moral Principle

KING ARTHUR! THE NAME CONJURES UP knights in armor, forbidden love, fleeting glory, and—of course—the quest for the Holy Grail, with hooves clattering and banners streaming. It brings with it the world of Camelot, and the feeling of acute nostalgia for a golden age that once was, but now seems out of reach forever.

These days, the name Arthur also brings to mind numberless books and television documentaries, each one promising to discover the real historical Arthur, and each one discovering a different Arthur. He was a Roman emperor; he was a Welsh warlord; he was a Celtic god; he was a Scythian legend; he was practically anything you can think of, because the tiny slivers of historical evidence are easy to fit into any theory, or to ignore if they don't fit.

It's a lot of fun to chase bits of historical evidence hither and yon, and to pounce on them when they seem to support our favorite theory. But to us, the historical truth about King Arthur is almost irrelevant. What's much more important is what people have believed about King Arthur for most of the last millennium and a half.

The story of King Arthur is the story of the creation of a terrestrial paradise—a paradise that was destroyed by sin. It is also a story of longed-for redemption, the hope that some miracle could restore the perfect world that sin had destroyed.

## The Biblical Theory of History

The Arthur of the Grail stories comes out of a definite historical period, and he carries with him a certain way of interpreting history. We might call it the biblical theory of history: this theory assumes that events are more than random occurrences, but have moral and spiritual meanings as well.

We see this mode of interpretation at work all through the Bible. The Old Testament writers interpret the long and tragic history of Israel according to simple moral principles. Every disaster is a judgment on the people's sins; every victory comes because the people have turned back to God. The whole reason for the stories of ancient kings and their battles is to show how God's providence works in the world.

When Corinthians started getting sick, St. Paul saw the same principle at work. The diseases plaguing them were not inexplicable events, or explicable only by physicians. They were brought on by disrespect for the body and blood of Christ, and they teach us a spiritual truth about the Eucharist—a truth that we should have learned already through the words of the Old Testament prophets.

A "cup" is a very common metaphor throughout the Psalms and the writings of the prophets, and it often is used to describe either the blessings or the curses that flow from God to his people.

If we remember no other verse from the Psalms, we remember "my cup runneth over" from Psalm 23 in the venerable King James Version. (Catholics who grew up with the Douay Version will remember it as Psalm 22.) It's a psalm of praise to God, who saves us from "the valley of the shadow of death," and the overflowing cup is a perfect image of the superabundance of God's blessing.

But the cup is not always a cup of blessing. "On the wicked he will rain coals of fire and sulfur," says Psalm 11:6; "a scorching wind shall be the portion of their cup."

Often in the prophets' writing the Lord's cup is "the cup of his wrath" (as in Isaiah 51:17). "Take from my hand this cup of the wine of wrath, and make all the nations to whom I send you drink it. They shall drink and stagger and go out of their minds because of the sword that I am sending among them" (Jeremiah 25:15–16).

Judgment came to Israel, just as the prophets had foretold. The northern kingdom of Israel (whose capital was Samaria) was conquered first. The prophet Ezekiel warned Judah, the southern kingdom, that it faced the same judgment:

> You shall drink your sister's cup,
>     deep and wide;
> you shall be scorned and derided,
>     it holds so much.
> You shall be filled with drunkenness and sorrow.
> A cup of horror and desolation
>     is the cup of your sister Samaria;
> you shall drink it and drain it out,
>     and gnaw its sherds,
>     and tear out your breasts;
> for I have spoken, says the Lord GOD. (Ezekiel 23:32–34)

The cup of God's blessing and the cup of his wrath are really the same thing. Psalm 75 is a hymn of praise, beginning "We give thanks to you, O God." God's judgment is one of the things for which we give thanks.

> For in the hand of the LORD there is a cup
>     with foaming wine, well mixed;
> he will pour a draught from it,

and all the wicked of the earth
>   shall drain it down to the dregs.
But I will rejoice forever;
>   I will sing praises to the God of Jacob.
All the horns of the wicked I will cut off,
>   but the horns of the righteous shall be exalted.
>       (Psalm 75:8–10)

We sing praise to God *because* he judges the wicked—which is the natural consequence of protecting and rewarding the righteous.

The wickedness of Israel and Judah brought catastrophic judgment, a tragic story of conquest, massacre, and exile.

The history of Britain is every bit as tragic as the history of Old Testament Israel, and the British saw their troubles in the same light. When catastrophe came, it was a judgment on the sins of the people. And catastrophe did come—the kind of catastrophe most civilized people can hardly imagine.

## Roman Britain

The green and pleasant island of Britain had already suffered multiple invasions by the time the Romans conquered it.

The earliest inhabitants may have been related to the present-day Basques. At some point in prehistory, they were invaded and subdued by a wave of Celts, the ancestors of the Irish and the Scots. Later on, those Celts were pushed back by another wave of Celts, the ancestors of today's Welsh and Bretons.

Then the Romans came.

About twenty years after the resurrection of Christ, Roman legions subdued Britain and made it a Roman province. Only in the far north did the unconquered Picts, descendants of the first wave of Celtic invaders, hold out.

Under the Romans, Britain was a civilized, prosperous, and largely peaceful place. In Rome, emperors were always being murdered, but it mattered much less who was emperor to a provincial Briton than it did to a senator in Rome.

The barbarian Picts were the only constant troublemakers. Every once in a while, they would launch a surprise raid on Roman Britain to pick up some loot and generally make nuisances of themselves. The Romans responded by building a great wall right across Britain to keep the Picts out. It worked most of the time, as long as the Romans kept a huge army stationed along the wall. That was the price Rome paid to keep Britain tranquil and safe.

In those peaceful years, the inhabitants of Britain led lives much like ours. They had well-built houses, with central heating to keep out the chilly northern climate. They fussed over their interior decorations and proudly showed off their expensive mosaic floors. They went shopping in town, or saw a play at the theater. They puttered in their gardens in the spring. Though most of the British still spoke their ancestral Celtic language, it was heavily peppered with Latin borrowings.

A Roman from anywhere else in the empire would feel right at home in Britain.

Roman Britain was, after all, just another part of the one big empire, and extensive commerce brought all kinds of people to the island. They brought news of the rest of the world with them, and as many ideas as goods were exchanged in the lively markets. When a new idea swept the empire, it couldn't take long to reach Britain.

## Christian Britain

We don't know how Christianity first came to Britain, but it must have been early in Christian history. There may have been Christians in Britain even before the Roman conquest: Britain had engaged in large-scale trade with other nations long before the conquest, and the Romans conquered the island precisely because it was too valuable to leave unconquered.

Whether Christianity came with Joseph of Arimathea bearing the Grail, or whether it came with a nameless sailor bearing nothing but the Good News, the British at the end of the Roman period believed Christianity had been there for a long time. The only historical account we have from the age of Arthur, a long rant against the sins of the people by sixth-century British historian St. Gildas the Wise, tells us that Christianity came to Britain during the

reign of Tiberius, who was emperor when Jesus was crucified. That Gildas could say so without fear of contradiction
shows that Christianity must have been well established in
Britain for longer than anyone could remember.

Archaeology tells us that Christianity and pagan-
ism lived side by side in Britain for quite a while,
just as they did in the rest of the empire. But when
Constantine the Great won the empire under the sign of
the cross (and Constantine, by the way, was in Britain
when he was proclaimed emperor in 306), Christianity
suddenly leaped from illegal cult to preferred religion
of the empire. By that time, a large portion of the
empire was already Christian; Constantine's decree of
religious tolerance was really only a belated announce-
ment that Christianity had won in spite of all attempts
to stamp it out. Though pagan superstition probably
lingered in the countryside, the organized religion of
Britain and the rest of the empire was Christianity by
the middle 300s.

## The Saxon Shore

Just as the Christian faith was taking firm hold in Britain,
a new barbarian threat began to appear on the eastern
coast of the island. At first it was a few pirate raids; then
the raids got bigger and the raiders better organized. It
was still a big job to keep the Picts confined to the northern reaches of the island. Now the Romans had Saxons to
deal with, too.

Saxons, as the Romans called them, came from the dark and little-explored forests of what we call Germany and Denmark. They worshiped pagan Germanic gods with names like Woden and Thunor. They had many different names for themselves, and a modern ethnologist would divide them into Angles, Saxons, Jutes, a few Frisians, and some other lesser divisions. Modern historians use the name "Anglo-Saxons" for the whole motley assortment of them, but eventually they would come to be known as English. (This can be confusing, because today we think of the English and the British as essentially the same group of people.)

By the end of the fourth century, the Romans had been forced to fortify the whole eastern shore of Britain—a massive undertaking that required a chain of forts linked by paved highways, so that any English raiders could be caught before they landed or cut off soon after. The whole operation was placed under the command of a count of the Saxon Shore, who was responsible for yet another gigantic army patrolling Britain.

The Romans were spending an enormous amount of resources to defend this distant island at the end of their empire. Green and pleasant as it might be, Britain was beginning to seem like more trouble than it was worth.

Meanwhile, weakened by civil war, economic depression, and the naked greed of the upper classes, the Roman Empire itself was collapsing. By the early fifth century, the Dark Ages were already casting their shadow across

Western Europe. As things got worse, the Roman soldiers who had guarded the frontiers of Britain were
called back to fight in various civil wars, or to guard
Rome itself from barbarian invasions. Naturally, the
barbarians surrounding Britain took every advantage of
the weakened defenses.

In 410, a committee from the British cities sent an
appeal to the emperor Honorius, asking for help in defend-
ing themselves. The barbarians threatened to overwhelm
the little defense force that was left. Honorius's answer
came by letter: Look to your own defense—I'm busy.

He was indeed busy. In that same year, the unthink-
able happened: the barbarian Goths invaded the city of
Rome. The inviolable city had been violated; it was clear
that no part of the empire was safe. With so much trouble
in the rest of the western empire, Rome was never again
strong enough to send soldiers to Britain. It wouldn't be
long before the empire in the west was gone completely;
only in the far-away eastern Mediterranean did a trun-
cated version of the Roman Empire survive.

## The Massacre

For what happened next, St. Gildas is our only source. Every
later historian follows his account more or less faithfully.

According to Gildas, in the absence of Roman
authority, the British fell into civil war and constant
bickering. Eventually, a strongman called Vortigern made
himself supreme commander and united the British

enough to fight off the Picts, who were once again erupting from the north.

Vortigern turned to an old Roman technique: fight barbarians with barbarians. His barbarian mercenaries were some English tribes (remember, they were Germanic barbarians) who could be bought with the promise of some supplies and a bit of land to settle on.

Vortigern's strategy worked: the Picts were beaten so soundly that the heart of Britain has never been successfully invaded from the north to this day.

The unfortunate by-product of the plan, however, was a large population of English warriors and their families to be taken care of. More of them were coming over in boats all the time. To the civilized British, who were used to all the amenities of Roman life—including regular baths—the English must have seemed a smelly, vicious, unkempt lot. And now that the Picts were defeated, why did the British need English deadbeats hanging about anyway?

So the British made their big mistake: they held back the supplies they had promised to their English allies. "We will break the treaty and plunder the whole island," the English warned them. The British suggested they go back where they came from.

It was just the opportunity the bored heathen warriors had been waiting for. The English suddenly erupted in a campaign of furious destruction and massacre that left most of Britain in ruins, especially the more settled eastern half. They spared no one, gleefully slaughtering young and old, male and female. They smashed down the comfortable Roman towns, crushing the inhabitants under the ruins of their own houses and churches. Our source, Gildas, described the horror, and his account sounds as though he heard it from eyewitnesses:

> All the columns were leveled with the ground by the frequent strokes of the battering ram, all the husbandmen routed, together with their bishops, priests, and people, whilst the sword gleamed, and the flames crackled around them on every side.
>
> Lamentable to behold, in the midst of the streets lay the tops of lofty towers, tumbled to the ground, stones of high walls, holy altars, fragments of human bodies, covered with livid clots of coagulated blood, looking as if they had been squeezed together in a press; and with no chance of being buried, save in the ruins of the houses, or in the ravening bellies of wild beasts and birds; with reverence be it spoken for their blessed souls, if, indeed, there were many found who were carried, at that time, into the high heaven by the holy angels. So entirely had the vintage, once so fine, degenerated and become bitter that, in the words of the prophet, there was hardly a grape or ear of corn to be seen where the husbandman had turned his back.[1]

Gildas was not at all sure of finding any "blessed souls" among the dead. He saw the barbarian outbreak as a judgment on the sins of the people, a nation that had degenerated so far from its ancient virtue that God's wrath justly fell on it.

Right here at the beginning of the story, we find that biblical principle that will follow us through all the Arthurian legends: events have meanings beyond themselves. Understanding history means not only knowing what happened and who caused it to happen, but also knowing *why* it happened, and what greater truth it teaches us.

## The Resistance

Life was grim for those who survived after the massacre by the English. The English continued to hunt down and kill the miserable refugees for some time afterward. Some, Gildas tells us, offered themselves as slaves to the English, seeing that their only other choices were starvation and massacre. Others left Britain entirely, forming a large British colony across the sea in northwestern Gaul—a place that soon flooded with so many British refugees that it was known as Little Britain, or (as we call it today) Brittany.[2] Still others found mountain havens and slowly began to regroup.

The English were still too few and too disorganized to hold the whole island. That gave the British the opportunity to organize a more effective resistance, and eventually they found a leader who turned the tide of the war. His name was Ambrosius Aurelianus, and Gildas has nothing but good things to say about him. To Gildas he was the last of the virtuous Roman Britons, the ideal model for the Christian warrior.

After Ambrosius, Gildas gives us no more names. As his chronicles approach his own time, Gildas simply makes offhand references to the history he assumes his audience knows firsthand. He tells us only that "after this, sometimes our countrymen, sometimes the enemy, won the field, to the end that our Lord might try in his accustomed manner these his Israelites, whether they loved him or not, until the year of the siege of Mount Badon."

Once again, we see Gildas interpreting British history the way Scripture interprets Israelite history. The victories and defeats are a long series of trials, like the book of Judges transplanted to the northern end of Europe.

The conclusion of the trials was the siege of Mount Badon. Gildas tells us nothing more about it, but it was evidently well known as the battle that ended the war. After that, the English barbarians were confined to their own small parcels of the island, and the British lived in peace until Gildas's time.

But who was the hero of Mount Badon? Gildas doesn't tell us. He didn't have to tell his original readers, since they knew the name well enough. We have to go to a source that may have been written hundreds of years later: the Annals of Wales, a compilation whose age is hotly debated. The Annals note:

The battle of Badon, in which Arthur bore the
cross of our Lord Jesus Christ on his shoulders for
three days and three nights, and the Britons were
the victors.

There he is: Arthur, the Christian warrior. Was that great
general who led the British to victory our legendary King
Arthur?

## Arthur

The answer is that he might have been. If the Annals of
Wales is not reliable evidence for the existence of Arthur,
it is at least evidence of what the Welsh believed sometime
early in the Middle Ages. By then it was regarded as a
known fact that Arthur was the victor in the battle of
Mount Badon.

He was more than just a great general. In this brief
notice, we get one other detail that's very illuminating:
"Arthur bore the cross of our Lord Jesus Christ on his
shoulders for three days and three nights."[3]

Arthur fought under the sign of Christ. That is the
only personal detail the annalist thinks is worth record-
ing about him.

It's a detail that speaks whole libraries about what
the descendants of Arthur's people believed. Arthur was
fighting for the survival of Christian civilization against
the looming pagan night. The story of Arthur is a story
about that battle. Arthur is more than a great leader who

saved the British from fierce invaders. He represents Christianity itself, fighting for its life against the forces of Satan.

In other words, we can already see Arthur as a sort of allegorical figure. He represents more than himself: he stands for an elemental conflict as old as time.

Now all we need is a mysteriously powerful dish or cup, and we'll have the basic ingredients for the stories of the Holy Grail.

## The Golden Age

Gildas remembers a time after the battle of Mount Badon when law and order had returned to the land.

> For as well the remembrance of such a terrible desolation of the island, as also of the unexpected recovery of the same, remained in the minds of those who were eyewitnesses of the wonderful events of both, and in regard thereof, kings, public magistrates, and private persons, with priests and clergymen, did all and every one of them live orderly according to their several vocations.[4]

Gildas wrote for a particular time and place, but history remembers him for good reason as St. Gildas the Wise. Like the Old Testament writers before him, Gildas sees history as a pattern of sin and judgment. Because God controls history, events have transcendent meanings. Since Gildas will be a primary source for every future historian of his time, his spiritual interpretation of history will permeate everything written about the last years of Roman rule in Britain. And we may call him wise for another reason as well: his direst prophecies did come true.

In the Annals of Wales, there is only one other mention of Arthur:

> Battle of Camlann, in which Arthur and Medraut perished; and there was plague in Britain and Ireland.

One interpretation of the Annals of Wales puts Camlann in the year 537; other historians, making various assumptions about the inaccuracy of the Annals' chronology, give wildly different dates. But according to the Annals, there was a space of twenty-one years between Badon and Camlann. That space could have been the age of order that Gildas remembered.

Somehow, the Arthurian golden age came to an end. Much later writers tell a dark and tragic tale: how Arthur was betrayed by his own son Mordred, and the two fell fighting against each other in a battle that ruined the kingdom. All the Annals say, however, is that Arthur and Medraut (Mordred) fell in the same battle. From Gildas, who wrote after Camlann (if Camlann really was a historical event), we know that the night had not fallen over Britain yet.

It would fall soon enough.

## The Darkness Falls

The rest of the story can be told briefly enough. Gildas's warning of impending ruin was all too prophetic. Divided by civil wars, ruined by shortsighted petty warlords, the British shortly lost the military advantage Arthur had left them. The English were quick to exploit British weakness. Less than a century after Arthur, most of Britain had fallen into English hands. Eventually the British who had not fled to Brittany were confined to the extreme western part of the island, where they became the unruly collection of insignificant kingdoms known to the English as Wales. There they mourned their loss for centuries in songs and stories.

In all the histories the Welsh wrote, they clung to Gildas's interpretation of their defeat: the sins of the people had brought judgment on Britain. And the treachery, luxury, carnality, and injustice cataloged by Gildas were not the worst sins of the British. Their worst sin was this: they had hated their English enemies so much that they had neglected the first duty of a Christian.

> Among other most wicked actions, not to be expressed, which their own historian, Gildas, mournfully takes notice of, they added this—that they never preached the faith to the Saxons, or English, who dwelt amongst them.[5]

These are the words of the first great English historian, St. Bede the Venerable, who lived in the late seventh and early eighth centuries. Across the centuries we can almost feel the hurt in his accusation: the British *could have* brought us the gospel—but they didn't! That neglect, Bede says, was the greatest sin of the British. The authors of the Grail romances would remember it.

For their sins, the British had been expelled from paradise. That was how they began to see their story: a creation and a fall. In the golden reign of Arthur, Britain had been a paradise, but sin destroyed that paradise, and the British were expelled from their Eden. They longed for a future redemption, a day when they might recover the island, perhaps led by Arthur himself, who—they said—was not dead, but sleeping.

And while he was sleeping, he dreamed—beautiful, fantastic dreams about a magical vessel so desirable that it was worth losing everything to possess it.

+

# Chapter the Sixth

## In Which King Arthur and His Best Knights Set Off on a Quest for a Magical Cauldron or Grail; with Observations on Grace and Nature

*Three shiploads full from Britain we set forth:*
*Save seven, none returned from Castle Siddi.*

A WELSH POEM FROM THE MIDDLE Ages tells the tale of a marvelous quest that Arthur and his best warriors undertook. The prize was a magical vessel—something so desirable that Arthur and his men were willing to lose their lives in the quest for it. It was called the Cauldron of the Chieftain of Annwfn.

We don't really know much about the story. "The Spoils of Annwfn," the poem that preserves it, is attributed to the legendary bard Taliesin, who was also one of Arthur's famous warriors. Taliesin tells the story from the point of view of an eyewitness, as though he himself had been among the few survivors of the quest. But the poem is obscure and allusive, obviously meant to be heard by people who already knew how the story went. So it's impossible to tell what really happened from the poem. We'd be in the same kind of predicament if all we knew about the War of 1812 came from "The Star-Spangled Banner."

The outline, however, is clear. Three shiploads of Arthur's best men, led by Arthur himself, set off on a quest for a magical vessel. Only seven men returned; the rest died in the aptly named Castle of Dangers.

## The Judgment of the Cauldron

And what did the few survivors have to show for all the dangers they faced and all the comrades they lost? The prize was a magical cauldron.

As far as we know, the only thing this cauldron did was boil food. But what it didn't do is really the most important thing. Any old pot will boil food, but any old pot will boil food for anyone. *This* cauldron refused to boil food for cowards. It exercised judgment: it rewarded the worthy and punished the unworthy.

Whether they realized it or not, the questing warriors were not looking for what the cauldron could give them. What they wanted was something it could not give them, something inside themselves: worthiness. They were willing to give up everything else to prove to themselves that they had it.

Now, no one believes that this is a true story about Arthur and his warriors. Or, at least (since, with Arthurian lore, there's always someone who believes just about any-thing) we can safely say that few serious scholars believe there is such a thing as a cauldron that will not boil a coward's food. What interests us, then, is not what the story says about Arthur and his men, but what it says about the people who told it and the people who heard it.

We can see that the idea of a quest for something unattainable had a powerful appeal for those who told and heard this story. When you come right down to it, it hardly mattered what the unattainable thing was. What mattered was the heroic quest itself.

Perhaps the people who told and heard this story did not believe that such a magical cauldron existed. But everyone could understand the longing for something that seems impossible to have.

## The Otherworld

Fragments of strange stories like this one have come down to us from those Dark Ages when the British had been reduced to a small collection of squabbling kingdoms known as Wales.

In these very early stories, of which we really only have bits and scraps, Arthur appears as a heroic warrior fighting his human enemies with almost (but not quite) super-human strength and courage. However, as Arthur began to represent the standard against which all heroes were measured, other stories collected around him—stories with their roots much further back in the misty Celtic past. There seems to have been a general feeling that all the best stories must have happened in Arthur's time, so all the legendary heroes of all ages began to gather in Arthur's court.

It was a strange and mysterious place, King Arthur's court. Magic and adventure were always just around the corner. In most of the Welsh stories, there was another world, dreamlike and magical, always just beyond our own and ready to materialize. Celtic scholars call this other world the Otherworld. The Welsh call it Annwfn.

The stories never mention the Otherworld as such. It's just that things happen that can be explained only by the hypothesis of a kind of parallel universe interrupting our own. Castles appear and disappear, magical ships show up at just the right time to take us to magical places, men emerge hale and hearty from eons of imprisonment. At any moment the Otherworld, supremely beautiful or supremely terrifying, may burst into our world, and we may have to deal with its hazy illogic. There's no highway to take you to the Otherworld, but it's never far away.

## Worthiness

There were other magical cauldrons in these ancient otherworldly tales. The poet Taliesin himself got his talent from a cauldron of knowledge and inspiration, according to one of the legends about him. It was an accident: he was watching somebody else's cauldron of knowledge when some of the hot boiling liquid splashed on his fingers. Instantly he stuck his fingers in his mouth to relieve the scalding pain, and the few drops he ingested were enough to give him all the knowledge in the world.

The same cauldron-of-knowledge story is told about other Welsh and Irish heroes, which shows that the story was well known and widely distributed. In Celtic legend, magical vessels could convey secret knowledge beyond mortal ken. This is a property we'll meet with again on our quest for the Holy Grail.

These magical vessels came in all shapes and with all kinds of different properties. In the bottles of Rhinnon Rhin Barnawd, milk would never turn sour. The basket of Gwyddneu Garanhir provided whatever food anyone desired, and enough for everyone who came to eat from it.[1] The idea of a vessel that gave you whatever food you wanted must have been powerfully appealing in an age when food was sometimes a rare commodity; at any rate, it's a common theme in Celtic lore, and the Welsh must have heard some version of the basket-of-plenty story. This, too, is a property we'll meet with again in the Holy Grail stories.

Objects that respond to the worth of the bearer are also common in Welsh legend. They were probably common in British legend before the British were Christians, and many of the Welsh stories seem to have originated in a pre-Christian world. Among the "Thirteen Treasures of Britain" (the Welsh were addicted to numbered lists) are several objects that reward worthiness and expose unworthiness.

- The sword Dyrnwyn, which would burst into flames when wielded by a true nobleman

- The Cauldron of Diwrnach the Giant, which (like the Cauldron of the Chieftain of Annwfn) boiled food for a brave man but not for a coward

- The Whetstone of Tudwal Tudlyd, which made a brave man's sword unfailingly deadly but had no effect on a coward's sword

- The Coat of Padarn Red-Coat, which would fit only a true nobleman[2]

With these objects, the worthiness rewarded is noble birth or courage in battle. But worthiness means something else to a Christian, and we'll discover that one of the remarkable features of the Grail romances is the way they take this common idea from Celtic legend and use it to destroy completely the old legends' notions of worthiness.

## Grace and Nature

For Christians, worthiness is something that comes as a grace from God, not some personal achievement to be demonstrated in battle. Without God's grace, no one can be truly worthy.

Now, it's an axiom of Christian theology that grace does not destroy nature, but rather builds on nature.

When we move from cauldrons and magic coats to the Holy Grail, we're not leaving this world and entering another. We're seeing an infusion of grace that transforms the things of this world into holy things

We see this truth illustrated in the sacraments, in which ordinary materials become the instruments of God's grace.

Baptism uses water, the most ordinary and common of all liquids. Baptism is so important that anyone—even a non-Christian—can perform it in an emergency, and water straight from the tap will do. Yet with simple, ordinary water, we are brought into the kingdom of Christ and made daughters and sons of God.

The elements of the Eucharist, too, are quite ordinary in themselves. No food is more common than bread, and it is a regrettable fact that most American churches use the cheapest wine they can find, mixed with perfectly ordinary water—ordinary, that is, in a material sense. Yet these are the materials that become the body and blood of Christ. In ordinary bread and cheap wine, we come face-to-face with God the Son.

Marriage likewise takes something natural and ordinary—the desire of men for women and of women for men—and transforms it into something incomparably greater: an image of Christ's love for his church, and even a participation in the inner life of the Trinity.

This is a very comforting truth: that God's grace is not far away in heaven, or beyond the sea, where we can never reach it (see Deuteronomy 30:11–14). Grace is as close to us as water, bread, and cheap red wine; as close as our own longing for something greater than what we have. Instead of denying nature, God's grace brings nature into his plan of salvation.

✝

# Chapter the Seventh

### In Which a Longing for a Lost Paradise Leads to the Rise of Medieval Civilization

THE DARK AGES WERE NOT UNIFORMLY dark. Here and there after the fall of Rome in 476, groups of monks copied manuscripts and kept some of the old learning alive. In Italy, some of the structure of Roman civilization remained, battered but not entirely dead. And in Britain, while those defeated by the invading English were themselves sinking further into barbarism, the English barbarians who had destroyed British civilization were nurturing a great civilization of their own.

## The Barbarians Tamed

The conversion of the English to Christianity was a special project of St. Gregory the Great, who was pope from 590 to 604. He sent a group of missionaries led by a rather timorous monk named Augustine (now known as

St. Augustine of Canterbury, not to be confused with the great theologian St. Augustine of Hippo). Since Augustine seemed unsure about how to proceed, Gregory sent specific instructions to the missionaries by an abbot who was traveling to Britain. It is worth reading Gregory's whole letter, which is short and remarkably practical:

> To his most beloved son, the Abbot Mellitus:
>
> Gregory, the servant of the servants of God.
>
> We have been much concerned, since the departure of our congregation that is with you, because we have received no account of the success of your journey. When, therefore, almighty God shall bring you to the most reverend Bishop Augustine, our brother, tell him what I have, upon mature deliberation on the affair of the English, determined upon, viz., that the temples of the idols in that nation ought not to be destroyed; but let the idols that are in them be destroyed; let holy water be made and sprinkled in the said temples, let altars be erected, and relics placed. For if those temples are well built, it is requisite that they be converted from the worship of devils to the service of the true God; that the nation, seeing that their temples are not destroyed, may remove error from their hearts, and knowing and adoring the true God, may the more familiarly resort to the places to which they have been accustomed.

And because they have been used to slaughter many oxen in the sacrifices to devils, some solemnity must be exchanged for them on this account, as that on the day of the dedication, or the nativities of the holy martyrs, whose relics are there deposited, they may build themselves huts of the boughs of trees, about those churches which have been turned to that use from temples, and celebrate the solemnity with religious feasting, and no more offer beasts to the devil, but kill cattle to the praise of God in their eating, and return thanks to the Giver of all things for their sustenance; to the end that, whilst some gratifications are outwardly permitted them, they may the more easily consent to the inward consolations of the grace of God.

For there is no doubt that it is impossible to efface everything at once from their obdurate minds; because he who endeavors to ascend to the highest place rises by degrees or steps, and not by leaps. Thus the Lord made himself known to the people of Israel in Egypt; and yet he allowed them the use of the sacrifices which they were wont to offer to the devil, in his own worship; so as to command them in his sacrifice to kill beasts, to the end that, changing their hearts, they might lay aside one part of the sacrifice, whilst they retained another; that whilst they offered the same beasts which they were wont to offer, they should offer them to God, and not to idols; and thus they would no longer be the same sacrifices.

This it behooves your affection to communicate to our aforesaid brother, that he, being there present, may consider how he is to order all things.

God preserve you in safety, most beloved son.


This is thoroughly pragmatic advice, and at the same time it shows a truly Christian spirit of tolerance. The people are used to coming to certain places for worship, so let them continue—but to worship the true God, not pagan idols. The people love their traditional feasts, so keep the feasts—and use them as opportunities to celebrate the new faith. The very things the people enjoy most about their pagan traditions can be the means of leading them to Christ.

As it happens, we have good evidence that Gregory's missionaries followed his advice—evidence that comes straight from the English language itself. In most European languages, the word for Easter comes from the root *pasch-*. But in English, "Easter" is the name of an old pagan spring festival. The name of the pagan festival didn't change, but the meaning of the festival changed completely. When we find that our traditional celebrations of Easter and Christmas seem to be rooted in ancient pagan festivals, we have Gregory to thank for preserving everything that was good in those traditions and turning it to the use of the Christian faith.

## The Vision of St. Gregory

The success of his missions might alone inspire us to call Pope Gregory a visionary. But Gregory is also famous for having miraculous visions, one of which became a great recurring theme of medieval art.

The story of this famous vision of St. Gregory is given a simple treatment in the *Golden Legend,* a medieval treasury of popular stories about saints:

It happened that a widow that was wont every Sunday to bring Hosts to sing Mass with, should on a time be houseled [have communion administered to] and communed. And when St. Gregory should give to her the holy Sacrament in saying: *Corpus domini nostri, etc.* (that is to say: The body of our Lord Jesus Christ keep thee into everlasting life), this woman began to smile before St. Gregory, and at once he withdrew his hand and put the Sacrament back upon the altar. And he asked her, before the people, why she smiled, and she said: Because the bread that I have made with my own hands thou namest the body of our Lord Jesus Christ.

At once St. Gregory put himself to prayer with the people, for to pray to God that hereupon he would show his grace for to confirm our belief, and when they were risen from prayer, St. Gregory saw the holy Sacrament in figure of a piece of flesh as great as the little finger of a hand, and anon after, by the prayers of St. Gregory, the flesh of the Sacrament turned into semblance of bread as it had been before, and therewith he communed and houseled the woman, who after was more religious, and the people more firm in the faith.

This miracle was a favorite subject for medieval artists, and in their paintings it became a bit more elaborate. St. Gregory, saying Mass, sees the figure of Christ himself rising from the altar, and a crowd around him witnesses the miracle. Sometimes the figure is a full-size man; sometimes it's a miniature, complete in every detail, but small enough to fit in the Holy Vessel.

In that latter form, the vision is an illustration of the truth every faithful Catholic already knows about the Eucharist: Christ is really present in the Eucharist; Christ really comes to us in body and blood. That image, a favorite with artists right up through the Renaissance, was so common—even painted on church walls—that it must have had some considerable influence on the way ordinary people thought about the Eucharist.

We'll see that image again, at the heart of the mystery of the Holy Grail.

## The Lost Civilization

The English Christians who owed their conversion to Gregory took to civilization rapidly and enthusiastically.

Soon they were exporting scholars to educate the rest of Europe. They were ready to answer the call when they were needed for the first grand attempt at restoring the civilization that had been lost.

The memory of Roman civilization had never entirely faded. Even three centuries after the last feeble western emperor had abdicated, the motley collection of barbarian states built on the ruins of the Western Empire acknowledged—in theory—the authority of the current emperor in Constantinople. In practice, of course, the eastern emperor had no power at all in the west, but the idea of the Roman Empire endured. Once again, western Europeans sensed that humanity had lived in paradise but had lost that paradise.

When Charlemagne, a Frankish king of the late 700s, took over the vast kingdom that had been left to him by his father (an area roughly corresponding to modern-day France and Germany), he was only barely literate. But he had an impossibly grand and ambitious idea: he would aim at nothing less than the restoration of Roman civilization. When Pope Leo III, recognizing the painfully obvious fact that the emperor in Constantinople had been unable to enforce his authority in the West for hundreds of years, crowned Charlemagne emperor of the West in 800,[1] it confirmed Charlemagne in his resolve to bring back Roman culture in his empire.

It was in England that Charlemagne found the intellectual resources he needed for his plan. Under the supervision of Alcuin, an English monk, the whole empire was given a crash course in civilization. Charlemagne demanded that all his nobles learn to read and write; he himself learned to read tolerably well, though his writing always cost him a great deal of effort and looked it. Monks were set to copying manuscripts at a prodigious rate. Under Alcuin, a new type of script was invented, specially designed to be easy to write and easy to read: it is the ancestor of the type in which this book is printed.

It was possibly the most gigantic civilizing effort in history, at least until the time of Peter the Great in Russia (1672–1725). And it was ultimately a failure. It simply wasn't possible to leap from barbarism to classical civilization in one generation.

But what a glorious effort it was! Alcuin's scholars copied everything they could find, and today the oldest surviving manuscripts of many classical works come from Charlemagne's time. The monks carefully restored Jerome's Vulgate translation of the Bible, which had been corrupted by copying errors over the centuries. Perhaps most important, they multiplied books to such an extent that the seed of literacy was planted for future generations. They sliced through the darkness and killed the Dark Ages. Europe was beginning to wake up.

## The Medieval Renaissance
By the time of the Norman Conquest, in 1066, Europe was on the brink of an intellectual explosion. During

the next century, almost everything we remember as great about medieval civilization blossomed. Aristotle had been rediscovered and was worming his way into the newly founded universities. Great philosophers such as Peter Abelard (1079–1142), Anselm (1033/34–1109), and Albertus Magnus (c. 1200–1280) were asking the most fundamental questions of philosophy and theology; Thomas Aquinas (c. 1224–1274) would soon take human reason to a peak from which, we might argue, everything since has been a descent. For the first time since the end of the Roman Empire in the West, Western Europe had a large population of educated men and women who were capable of understanding intellectual subtleties.

Also for the first time, writers began to use vernacular language for serious literature. It was a symptom of the rise of literacy: no longer was reading limited to a tiny clerical class. French, English, and German all became serious literary languages at about the same time.

Women made up a large number not only of the readers but also of the writers. Women wrote in every genre, from popular romance to the most refined mysticism. Quite suddenly, women had earned the right to have intellectual lives of their own. And men paid attention to what they had to say.

The number of women writers in the Middle Ages is surprising, especially when we have an almost complete lack of women's writings from classical antiquity. It's hard to account for this sudden wave of literary women by any one cause. Certainly the church had something to do with it. Large numbers of women in religious houses were learning to read and write: for the first time groups of women were being educated as a deliberate institutional policy. Social life had also changed: women were included in the feasts and entertainments that formerly had been for men only.

The outbreak of female literacy had at least two important effects on the literature of the age. One was that compositions by women were reaching large audiences and thus having a noticeable influence on compositions by men. The other—and this one was even more important—was that women made up a large part of a writer's audience. If the tale was not pleasing to the women in the audience, the author might never be asked to tell another one. So writers were composing stories with women readers in mind.

All these readers, male and female, demanded books, and where there is a demand for books, writers are never slow to pick up their pens. The best productions spread across Europe from court to court (feudal Europe had a lot of courts) as fast as the copyists could reproduce them. For the first time since the end of the classical era, it was possible for a writer to become something of a literary celebrity in his or her own lifetime.

Most writers, however, never gained much of a reputation outside their own countries. They wrote for their own amusement or—probably more often—for the amusement of a wealthy patron. No one actually made a living as a writer, but amusing a wealthy patron was a very good way to advance one's career in the church or in the government.

And every once in a while, some writer, either by cleverness or by accident, hit on exactly what the reading public wanted. The result was the medieval equivalent of a runaway international best seller, spreading to all the courts of Europe and spawning a host of imitations. It would be hard to think of a better example than the *History of the Kings of Britain*.

## The Perfect Action Blockbuster

Whenever I have chanced to think about the history of the kings of Britain, on those occasions when I have been turning over a great many such matters in my mind, it has seemed a remarkable thing to me that, apart from such mention of them as Gildas and Bede had each made in a brilliant book on the subject, I have not been able to discover anything at all on the kings who lived here before the incarnation of Christ, or indeed about Arthur and all the others who followed on after the Incarnation. Yet the deeds of these men were such that they deserve to be praised for all time. What is more, these deeds were handed joyfully down in oral tradition, just as if they had been committed to writing, by many peoples who had only their memory to rely on.

That was how Geoffrey of Monmouth introduced his *History of the Kings of Britain,* a book that burst on the scene in the early 1100s. It would be a book about the great deeds of the kings of Britain; it would tell stories that simply aren't to be found in other books, and in particular it would tell stories of Arthur. It seems that people were looking for a book just like this one. Geoffrey's book turned into a literary sensation of which it would be hard to find an equal before the Harry Potter series.

What made the *History* so wildly popular?

For one thing, Geoffrey's book is full of battle scenes, and many of them are masterpieces of their genre. He takes particular delight in clever stratagems, and he can certainly turn out a noble speech with the best of them. The battles themselves are described with admirable clarity, so that we never have any trouble following the action. And all the elements are perfectly balanced: never too many speeches, never too much blood, never too much suspense, but always everything in just the right proportion.

In short, Geoffrey was an entertainer who crafted the perfect action blockbuster.

The *History* is an inexhaustible fund of great stories. King Lear and Cymbeline made their first literary appearances there. But Shakespeare wasn't the only playwright to find inspiration in Geoffrey's pages. The popular play *Gorboduc* also came from a story in the *History,* and Old King Cole still lives in nursery rhyme. Geoffrey's influence on literature as a whole, beyond just writings on Arthur, was enormous.

Whatever the reason, his book was an instant hit. And one measure of how large the secular audience for books had become is the fact that Geoffrey was soon translated from Latin into vernacular languages—even Welsh, the language of the remnant population of the British so decimated by the barbarous English half a millennium before.

"Translating" in the Middle Ages was a much freer art than it is today. Translators didn't mind adapting, summarizing, or expanding the original as they saw fit. The two most famous translations of Geoffrey—by Wace into Norman-French rhyme and by Layamon into Middle English—both add some details not found in Geoffrey's account. Wace, in particular, added a certain Round Table, around which King Arthur's famous knights sat so that no one of them would be more honored than the others. It was a detail he probably got from Breton storytellers; at any rate, the Round Table would soon become almost as much a character in the Arthurian romances as the people who sat around it.

## In Love with the Eucharist——but Ignorant of Doctrine

Just as Europe was falling in love with the stirring tales of Arthur's court, another popular movement was rolling across the continent with similar speed and power.

By the mid-thirteenth century, Europe would add to the Christian calendar a new celebration, the Feast of Corpus Christi.

The Eucharist had always been the object of keen devotion among Christians. But just about the time Geoffrey of Monmouth was writing, that devotion started to show signs of becoming something more than keen. It was beginning to inspire the sort of popular movement that modern politicians like to call a *groundswell*.

Like St. Gregory in the late sixth century, ordinary men and women—children, too—of every class and condition saw the Host transformed into a lamb, or into a child, or saw a child enter the Host. Some of these visionaries were simple peasants. Some were kings: Edward the Confessor (c. 1003–1066), the last English king of the illustrious line of Alfred the Great, saw a child in the hands of the archbishop of Canterbury at Mass. Sometimes the Host miraculously pointed out a blasphemer; sometimes it gave miraculous protection against fire or shipwreck.

During that period, women's mystical experiences were taken seriously—and thus recorded—so we know that seeing a child in the Host was an especially common experience among religious women. Some especially ascetic types were miraculously sustained by the Eucharist alone, rejecting all other food; this was another religious experience that seems to have been most typically female.[2]

We don't have to decide whether or not we believe in any of these miracles. From our point of view, the important fact is that they were widely believed and reported. The whole atmosphere of the age was charged with a lively sense of the real presence. It wasn't the result of heavy propaganda from the church, either; on the contrary, it was lay believers who finally pushed the church to institute the new Feast of Corpus Christi.

Nor was this sense of the real presence a mere abstraction or private religious feeling. It was a movement that bore fruit. This was also the age of the first hospitals in medieval Europe, an age that saw homes founded for poor widows and orphans. As the noted medievalist Miri Rubin points out, this burst of institutional charity came just as Eucharistic piety was reaching its peak. It was impossible to be so keenly aware of the body of Christ in the Eucharist without being just as keenly aware of the body of Christ in the poor and helpless.

Along with this sense of the real presence came an equally lively sense of the holiness of the Eucharist and the importance of receiving it worthily. In many of the miracle stories, the Host identifies a mortal sinner. For most ordinary people, receiving the Eucharist was a rare event; it was normal, in fact, to receive it only once a year, at Easter. At other times, merely contemplating the Blessed Sacrament with the eyes was thought to be almost as sustaining. The church sometimes had to remind people that it was still necessary to partake of the Eucharist, not just to look at it, however devotedly. The Fourth Lateran Council (1215) required all Christians to confess and take communion at least once a year, at Easter, and the council would not have made such a requirement if the practice were already universal.

Of course, we have to remember that we're speaking mostly of ordinary people, and specifically of the religiously inclined among them. Even in the Age of Faith—as the Middle Ages are often called today—there was an appalling ignorance of the faith among the laity, and even the clergy. That same Lateran Council tried to set in motion a gigantic effort to educate the laity in the fundamentals of the faith, but it was an uphill struggle. Ignorance had put down firm roots in the last few hundred years. Bishops who surveyed their dioceses were shocked to find how little the revival of learning had seeped down from the courts. In some of the parishes none of the laypeople seemed to know even the Lord's Prayer, and the parish priests were scarcely any better informed. Some of them knew nothing at all of Latin, the learned language of the church and the liturgy. On the other hand, many a bishop never visited his diocese in his life, having been appointed to the see because of his family connections. In many places, most people simply didn't go to church at all. A survey of medieval parish churches shows that the buildings were far too small to hold more than a tiny fraction of their parish populations. When people did go to church, they often treated the place like a public market, shouting and carrying on while the Mass was being said—possibly by a priest who had no idea what he was saying.[3]

The problem was not easy to solve. By 1281, the English bishops were still trying to implement a program that would teach the laity the basics: the Our Father, the Hail Mary, and the Apostles' Creed. Over and over, the best minds in the church posed themselves the same question: how can we bring Christ to the laity—since so many of them aren't coming to us? As late as 1551, one bishop found that a large number of priests couldn't answer the question "Who is the author of the Lord's Prayer?"[4]— roughly the religious equivalent of that old game-show favorite, "Who is buried in Grant's tomb?"

It was an age of strange contrasts: some of the greatest minds in the history of thought lived side by side with priests who couldn't recite the Lord's Prayer—the most refined mystics with coarse and ignorant louts.

Even the monasteries, which had been so successful in preserving what was left of civilization, were hardly immune to the problems of the age.

In spite of occasional Viking raids and other disasters, the monasteries had succeeded in creating islands of peace and stability in Europe. It was not at all unusual for wealthy nobles, even kings, to retire to a monastery after an active public life of pillage, bringing a large part of their wealth with them. Since monks were sworn to poverty, the riches became common property. After a few centuries, some monastic houses were really filthy rich—and some monks were deeply troubled by the obvious dissonance between their vow of poverty and their palatial surroundings.

## Strong Medicine for Weak Faith

In response, then, to the widespread ignorance of Christian practices and beliefs, and the increasing worldliness of even those vowed to the religious life, reform movements swept through the monastic world in waves. As early as 1098, the Cistercians began their campaign to reform the monastic life. Just as the first monks had withdrawn from the world, so the Cistercians withdrew from the worldliness of the established orders. St. Bernard of Clairvaux (1090–1153) joined the young community and soon became its leader and inspiration.

The Cistercians produced, or perhaps attracted, some of the brightest minds of the age, and before long there was a distinctly Cistercian school in theology—a fact that delighted the Cistercians. Aside from St. Bernard, one of the leading lights of Cistercian theology was William of Saint-Thierry (c. 1085–c. 1148), a friend and biographer of St. Bernard. Says the medievalist Dom Jean Leclercq:

> William's whole teaching is the history of the soul's ascent from sin to union and oneness with God, until it is moved by the influence of the Spirit alone. Then in faith it has a foretaste of the beatific vision. . . . In his teaching, which is not merely theoretical, an important place is taken by the Scriptures and the sacraments, chiefly the Holy Eucharist, through which we come to Christ.[5]

We will see this teaching—of the soul's journey, the beatific vision, and the quest rewarded—at the heart of the best Grail legends and romances.

The Cistercian life was in no way "merely theoretical." Manual labor was an essential part of their asceticism. Nor did the Cistercians simply withdraw from the world and leave it to its fate. Missionary work was one of their strengths. Fighting heresy was an especially important cause to them. St. Bernard's preaching brought back many souls into the orthodox church when various heresies were springing up here and there—not an uncommon occurrence when ignorance abounds.

St. Bernard also supported and advised the new military orders. The Knights Templars and the Knights Hospitallers were, in effect, knightly monks, or monkish knights. Their mission was to protect the peace of Christendom; in practice, that usually meant fighting the Muslims in Spain and in the Holy Land. The idea of Christian warriors was certainly nothing new: Arthur himself, after all, had often been portrayed as the paragon of the Christian warrior, carrying the image of the Virgin Mary into battle. But for the first time, large groups of men were making a sincere attempt to be *purely* Christian warriors, taking upon themselves much of the same discipline and asceticism that monks committed themselves to, but devoting their lives to actively protecting the weak and helpless.

Again, here we have a pattern for the ideal knight, who will appear in stories of the legendary Grail.

Most knights, however, were still of the worldly type. Many of them were only nominally Christian. Their main concerns were their own ambitions—glory in battle, wealth, and of course the admiration of the ladies. Especially the ladies. As women took on more and more importance in social life, their love was more and more important to a man's perception of his own success. That often gave women more dignity and value, but on the other hand it also led to some strange excesses. In some European courts, it seemed almost as though Christianity was being replaced by a new official religion, a cult in which the only god was love.

It was an irony that was hard to appreciate in its own time, when the battle lines were being drawn. The Christian Church had in many ways saved classical civilization; now classical civilization was back with a vengeance, bringing along with it a neo-pagan cult of love that threatened to replace Christianity in courtly life.

✝

# Chapter the Eighth

## In Which the World Goes Mad for Love

THE LITERATE NOBILITY AND SUB-NOBILITY OF the High Middle Ages demanded splendid entertainments, and some of the most splendid entertainments in the French language came from the pen of a woman we know as Marie de France. She was one of those great female literary figures who became increasingly common in the Middle Ages, and her specialty was enthralling stories of love and magic.

Marie tells us that she had first thought of adapting some story from the Latin. But anybody could do that. So instead she took her stories from an inexhaustibly fertile source: the Breton minstrels.

> The tales whose truth I know so well,
> Which often I've heard Bretons tell,
> Now briefly I'll relate to you.[1]

Tales of Arthur had probably been part of the common heritage of the Welsh and the Bretons since the battle of Mount Badon. Yet there was also something new in these Breton tales—something that didn't rise from the mists of ancient Celtic lore. These are love tales, deeply marked by that complex of ideas that modern medievalists call "courtly love."

## Love and Etiquette

"Courtly love" is a staple of classes in medieval literature, and more than one textbook has given a numbered list of rules for the game. It involves a forbidden affair carried on by nobles, driven by passion, and almost always adulterous. But it's important to remind ourselves that the term *courtly love* is a nineteenth-century invention. It was created in the 1880s by the medievalist Gaston Paris to describe certain common characteristics he observed in medieval literature.

Since then, generations of students have graduated with the impression that "courtly love" was a game of acting out that medieval lords and ladies played—something like paintball with lutes.

In fact, the medieval romances and the treatises on love were describing what the authors believed they had observed about the workings of the human heart, as channeled through the etiquette of a medieval court. It is true that some of them took up love as a game; in every generation, love is a game for a certain type of person.

And the medieval writers were intimately familiar with Ovid, the ancient Roman poet whose *Art of Love* occupied a back shelf in every well-stocked medieval library. But most of the medieval romances describe characters whose emotions were supposed to be sincere and overwhelming. The most popular romances were successful not because they followed the rules of a game, but because they seemed true to the movements of the heart—the same movements their audiences felt in their own hearts.

Most of those movements of the heart are the same ones we feel today. We still fall in love—sometimes recklessly, as a glance at the police blotter will confirm. We still feel our hearts beat faster at the sight of our beloved; we still feel the urge to prove our love, if only by buying expensive jewelry.

But some things have changed. Even in our fairly lax age, it comes as a bit of a shock to us to see how lightly—or even how approvingly—some of the medieval romances treat adultery. The idea that a woman should find her true love long after she has been married seems perfectly normal to the knights and ladies in some of these stories. Generally the young woman's husband is an old grump, and that alone is all the justification she needs for giving her love, and everything else, to the first attractive knight who comes along. Of course, since there is no possibility of divorce, the knight may have to kill the husband in battle before we can have a happy ending. But the husband deserves it for being such an old grump.

In the early centuries of the church, during the age of the church fathers, adultery was one of the three sins considered beyond the limit of sacramental forgiveness (the others were apostasy and murder). Some churches would grant sacramental forgiveness and the Eucharist if the penitent was in danger of imminent death. Spiritual writers did not rule out God's forgiveness for these sins, but they held that the church had no right to absolve the big three. The sinner was expected to spend a lifetime in penance.

By the High Middle Ages, however, adulterous love was one of the most important themes of the minstrels' tales, and it would turn into one of the great themes of medieval literature. Sometimes the tale was dark and tragic. But just as often there was a happy ending—happy, at least, for the lovers, though the husband often wound up at the pointy end of a lance.

## The Perversity of Age

Marie de France was certainly one of the great propagators of these modern notions of love. We can take her ballad *Guigemar* as a typical example. The heroine is "a lady of high birth. She was noble, courtly, beautiful, and wise." Her husband, of course, is "a very old man," and naturally he's of a jealous disposition. He's so jealous, in fact, that he keeps her locked up in a garden with only one entrance, guarded night and day. (The garden, however, is open to the sea, which will prove the nasty old man's undoing.) "All old men," Marie explains helpfully, "are jealous and hate to be cuckolded. Such is the perversity of age." On the other hand, in the light of what happens to him, the old man's precautions seem understandable if not forgivable.

The husband has taken care to make his wife's surroundings pleasant, imprisoning her in "a chamber of incomparable beauty." Paintings of Venus are all over the walls. But the paintings are meant to be instructive as well as beautiful: "In the painting Venus was shown as casting into a blazing fire the book in which Ovid teaches the art of controlling love and as excommunicating all those who read this book or adopted its teachings."

It's hard to imagine how the artist painted a mass excommunication. But the image of Venus flinging Ovid's book into a blazing fire is vivid enough. We can hear the low rumble of murmurs and snickers rolling through the audience: they've all read Ovid's book, and they know exactly why the ugly old man felt the way he did about it.

So we have a beautiful young woman imprisoned by an ugly old husband. All we need now is a handsome young knight, and the powers of the Otherworld are quick to provide him. A wounded knight named Guigemar steps aboard a mysterious empty ship and is magically whisked straight to the young lady's secret bower. She nurses him back to health, and of course they find true love—a love that Marie seems to consider laudable and correct: "A loyal partner once discovered should be served, loved, and obeyed."

The lady and her knight spend a year and a half serving, loving, and obeying each other in a horizontal position. But eventually the husband, suddenly recalling that he has a beautiful young wife stashed away somewhere, makes the long-overdue discovery. Guigemar is sent back in the ship that brought him, and the lovers are separated for a long time. At last, however, the same magical ship reappears to offer the young lady a means of escape. She takes her opportunity, and when the ship lands she disembarks in the territory belonging to a man named Meriaduc, who takes a fancy to her—so much so that when Guigemar shows up and recognizes his love, Meriaduc refuses to give her up.

But everything ends happily when Guigemar besieges Meriaduc's castle and kills him. "With great joy he took away his beloved. Now his tribulations were over," Marie explains.

"But wait a minute," we might ask: "isn't she still married to the ugly old man?"

Well, technically, she might be. But it doesn't seem to worry anybody. Marie doesn't even bother to tell us what happened to him. True love trumps loveless marriage any old day.

## Love as Heresy

Marriage seems altogether irrelevant to Marie. In the ballad *Equitan,* adulterous lovers end up dead, and Marie warns us that "anyone willing to listen to reason could profit from this cautionary tale." But it's not adultery per se that we're being warned against. The lovers in the tale wickedly plot to kill the inoffensive husband and are caught in their own trap.

In the ballad *Lanval,* the title character finds true love with an otherworldly beauty. Two lines of dialogue after their first sight of each other, "she granted him her love and her body." When the expected complications are resolved (including some advances from Arthur's queen that Lanval has to rebuff), he rides off to spend the rest of his life with her on the magical island of Avalon. There's no mention of whether the lovers ever married, but clearly that's because we're not expected to care. The lovers are together, and nothing else matters.

All this seems pretty far from the Christian ideal of marriage, and certainly directly opposed to the deep and sincere piety that also flourished in many medieval hearts. No wonder some modern writers analyze courtly love as a species of heresy: if these newfangled ideas of love were taken seriously, then they were in direct contradiction to what the church taught about the sacrament of marriage. Not only that, but they also set up love as a kind of god. In the world of *Guigemar* and *Lanval,* all things are judged by romantic love alone.

All this casual adultery brings to mind the old pagan fertility cults, and it's hardly surprising to hear the medieval love-cultists invoking the name of Venus, the classical goddess of letting the good times roll. Courtly love really does begin to look like a religious movement, and soon we'll see its devotees adopting shockingly religious language.

This was indeed an age of strange contrasts. It was almost as though ignorance and wisdom, piety and impiety were reaching their peaks at the same time. The best minds of the church were wondering how to bring the basic truths of the Christian faith to the ignorant masses. But how much more of a problem the nobility would be! With the masses, mere ignorance was the enemy. With the nobility, the church would have to conquer Ovid!

*Lanval* is set in the court of King Arthur, and Marie includes the Round Table as a well-known part of the setting. Adultery seems to have been the national sport of Britain in King Arthur's time, to judge by the tales the romancers told. One love affair in particular occupied more pages of romance than any of the others—it caught and held the imaginations of the medieval audience as no other love affair had, and it still has a hold on our imaginations today.

## The Poet of Adultery

Another Marie, the countess of Champagne, considered herself one of the world's leading authorities on the subject of love. Her court was famous for its sophisticated entertainments, and one of the most reliable providers of those entertainments was Chrétien de Troyes—a French poet of the 1100s who would go down in history as one of the great storytellers of all time.

Chrétien's favorite subject was King Arthur's court. Or perhaps it was Marie's favorite subject, for in one of Chrétien's most famous tales, he tells us that Marie herself commissioned the work and gave him the subject for it: "Here Chrétien begins his book about the Knight of the Cart. The material and the treatment of it are given and furnished to him by the countess, and he is simply trying to carry out her concern and intention."[2]

In the story *The Knight of the Cart,* Arthur's queen, Guinevere, has been abducted. On his way to attempt the queen's rescue, Gawain, the king's nephew, meets an unknown knight who has worn out his horse. He follows the knight long enough to see him encounter a cart. The knight, walking behind the cart, sees a dwarf in the driver's seat and calls out to him, "Dwarf, for God's sake, tell me now if thou hast seen my lady, the queen, pass by here."

The dwarf simply replies, "If thou wilt get up into the cart I am driving thou shalt hear tomorrow what has happened to the queen."

Obviously our nameless knight is trying to rescue Queen Guinevere. He faces a dilemma, however; the cart, at this time, served the same purpose as a pillory, in that it was used to display wrongdoers and lawbreakers. To ride in such a cart was to bring upon oneself shame that could not be erased. It was a permanent social smear. What should the knight do now? To mount the cart would be to bring everlasting shame upon himself; not mounting it might mean passing up his only chance of finding the queen.

> The knight hesitated only for a couple of steps before getting in. Yet it was unlucky for him that he shrank from the disgrace, and did not jump in at once; for he will later rue his delay. But common sense, which is inconsistent with love's dictates, bids him refrain from getting in, warning him and counseling him to do and undertake nothing for which he may reap shame and disgrace. Reason, which dares thus speak to him, reaches only his lips, but not his heart; but love is enclosed within his heart, bidding him and urging him to mount at once upon the cart. So he jumps in, since love will have it so, feeling no concern about the shame, since he is prompted by love's commands.[3]

Love! This is the first we've heard of it, but it appears that the unknown knight has more than selfless motives for finding Guinevere.

Chrétien is a master storyteller. He lets us know just enough to keep us riveted to his narrative but never too much to spoil a surprise. He manages to tell half his story without even revealing the knight's name. We know him only as the Knight of the Cart, and everywhere he goes, the shame of that cart follows him. But at last, after many thrilling adventures, he reaches the castle where the queen is held captive. There, already weakened by his prodigious feats of knightly boldness, he confronts the wicked Meleagant, who holds the queen and many other captives from Arthur's kingdom. If the knight defeats Meleagant, all the captives will go free. But Meleagant is one of the best fighters in the world, though also one of the wickedest knights, and our nameless hero gets the worst of it.

> But up at the window of the tower there was a wise maiden who thought within herself that the knight had not undertaken the battle either on her account or for the sake of the common herd who had gathered about the list, but that his only incentive had been the queen; and she thought that if he knew that she [the queen] was at the window seeing and watching him, his strength and courage would increase. And if she had known his name, she would gladly have called to him to look about him.
>
> Then she came to the queen and said: "Lady, for God's sake and your own as well as ours, I

beseech you to tell me, if you know, the name of yonder knight, to the end that it may be of some help to him."

"Damsel," the queen replies, "you have asked me a question in which I see no hate or evil, but rather good intent; the name of the knight, I know, is Lancelot of the Lake."

Lancelot—so that's his name! Now, of course, we modern readers know who we're dealing with. The story of Lancelot and Guinevere is almost an archetype of forbidden love in Western culture. Chrétien's readers probably knew the name, too.[4] But Chrétien's *Knight of the Cart* is the earliest version of Lancelot's story that survives.

Once Lancelot, inspired by the sight of his love, has defeated Meleagant, the prisoners are all free to go, and we might suppose that the story is over. Actually, we're only half done.

For one thing, Chrétien still has to treat us to a love scene. When Lancelot visits the queen in her chamber at night, "he comes to the bed of the queen, whom he adores and before whom he kneels, holding her more dear than the relic of any saint." And after a night of pleasure, "it cost him such pain to leave her that he suffered a real martyr's agony." Here we have an act of adultery deliberately described in Christian religious terms. This is almost beyond heretical, because it seems to turn Christian morality on its head.

## The Cult of Love

But why use religious language? Was it really a ploy among the romance writers to demean the Christian faith? Or was something deeper at work here? Perhaps the religious language comes naturally in love stories because what the devotees of love are actually longing for is a religious experience. They expect something so mind-shatteringly intense that it changes the whole direction of their lives. All they end up getting is sex, but in their deepest selves they want something that is beyond what sex can provide.

Like most heresies, courtly love is based on a twisted truth.

Love may seem for a while like the answer to all the questions we've been asking. But even human love, great and powerful and mysterious as it is, is too small to fill that hole in our hearts. Sexually thrilling, emotionally charged romantic love is not our destination after all; yet that desire sets us in the direction of the real thing, the ultimate Love. This is the principle that many of the great medieval romance writers seem to have missed. It does appear that the writer Chrétien didn't miss it completely, as we'll see in one of his later romances.

The rest of the story, in effect, deals with how Lancelot and Guinevere successfully cover up their affair—always a necessity when the lady's husband is as well armed as Arthur is. There is no suggestion of regret on the part of Lancelot for betraying his lord, or on the part of Guinevere for betraying her husband. Guinevere and Lancelot may continue their secret pleasures, and Arthur may continue, happy in the delusion that he has a faithful wife. Everybody wins.

Is that a satisfying ending? It probably was to Countess Marie, and Chrétien (professional entertainer that he was) gave his patroness what she wanted. But the idea of carefree adultery with no consequences might be a little disturbing to someone with a sincerer attachment to the Christian faith. It might even have been a little disturbing to Chrétien—that might account for his disclaimer at the beginning that "the material and the treatment of it are given and furnished to him by the countess, and he is simply trying to carry out her concern and intention."

We can imagine sincere Christian thinkers bemoaning the depraved state of popular entertainment, just as they do today. But what can be done about it? Popular entertainment is popular because it's good at entertaining people. Preachers can preach till they're blue in the face, but all the sermons in the world won't stop most people from listening to the stories they like to hear.

There is, however, an alternative to preaching—an alternative that could be described, in the best sense, as perversion. As Gregory the Great had advised his missionaries centuries before, the Christian faith wins hearts most easily if it adapts itself to the people's customs and habits. If the people like colorful adventure stories, what's to prevent the true Christian faith from coming to them that way? Surely Christianity could find a champion or two among the romancers. Gregory's advice had proved extraordinarily effective in making Christians out of pagans; now it was time to try the same methods in making real Christians out of the disciples of Ovid.

# Chapter the Ninth

## In Which We Go Looking for Love and Find the Grail

S OMETIME AFTER HE WROTE THE REST of his famous Arthurian romances, Chrétien de Troyes started work on a new one with a new subject. He called it *The Story of the Grail,* and he dedicated it not to Countess Marie but to Count Philip of Flanders. And although it starts out looking like yet another tale of adventure and courtly love, it winds up taking quite an unexpected direction.

### Mother Knows Best

We begin in the spring, when the trees are blooming and the birds are singing and the poets are carefully transcribing all the natural phenomena for later use at the beginnings of romances, which almost always begin in the spring. Deep in the forest, the only son of a widow rides out from his secluded home and hears a sound he

has never heard before: the sound of five knights march-
ing in full armor, with all the clinking and banging and
rattling that wood and steel create.

> The young man heard but did not see
> The men approaching rapidly.
> He marveled at the sound, and said,
> "My lady mother, by my head,
> Spoke truly: devils are the most
> Horrific things the world can boast.
> She said to cross myself if I
> Should meet a devil passing by.
> But devils I won't hold in dread:
> I scorn to cross myself. Instead,
> I'll strike the strongest of the lot
> With this sharp javelin I've got.
> Then I'll have nothing more to fear:
> The others will not dare come near."

In one little soliloquy, Chrétien neatly sums up his young
hero's two leading characteristics: he is a naïf who misin-
terprets almost everything, and he relies entirely on his
own courage and strength.

From the noise the knights make, the young man
assumes they must be devils. But then he catches sight of
them, and he knows he was mistaken.

He said, "Lord God, mercy on me!
These must be angels that I see.
Alas! How I was made to sin,
And oh! how very wrong I've been
To say that they were devils. See,
My mother did not lie to me
In telling me that angels are
The loveliest things there are by far,
Excepting God himself alone.
And this one must be God, I own,
For he's so fair to look upon
He beats the others ten to one.
And since my mother furthermore
Told me to worship and adore
And honor God, that's what I'll do
To this one, and the others too."

We can imagine that by this time, Chrétien's audience was practically rolling in the aisles. The idea of mistaking a group of knights for God and his angels must have been very funny to an audience full of knights. They might have whispered to each other that the young man's first impression was more accurate.

Obviously, the young man knows nothing of the outside world. In fact, he doesn't even know his own name. Apparently, with only his mother for company, he never needed any name other than "Son." That gives Chrétien another chance to use the trick that worked so well in *The Knight of the Cart:* he withholds his hero's name from us until halfway through the story.

But Chrétien's narrative isn't just for laughs: he's developing his hero's character and the plot at the same time. Over and over again, our young naïf will get very good advice and—with the best intentions—completely misapply it in the real world. The whole story will turn on that failure in his personality.

As soon as he discovers what the knights really are, of course our young protagonist wants to be one. That's very bad news for his poor old mother. She had a good reason for bringing him up deep in the forest, and now for the first time she tells him. His father and both his brothers had been knights, but both brothers had been killed in battle, and the father died of grief at the news. The young man's mother thought she could keep him from ever even hearing of chivalry, and thus preserve her one remaining son from the fate of his brothers. But chivalry is simply too pervasive. It has found him at last, and now it will take him from her just as it did his brothers.

The young man's mother gives him some last advice— advice that we already know he will distort in a comical fashion. Always serve ladies in need, she tells him, and a kiss from such a lady is a great prize—but never take more than a kiss. If she loves you enough to give you her ring, it is proper to wear it. Finally, go to church and pray. This last part has to be explained more thoroughly: our young man has grown up so far off the beaten track that he has never seen a church.

We expect comedy, and our boy doesn't disappoint us: his misadventures on the way to Arthur's court must have earned Chrétien quite a few belly laughs from the audience. At his first sight of a noble lady, he manages to steal her ring and twenty sloppy kisses—all the while believing he's following his mother's wise advice. It might not be so funny to the lady or her insanely jealous lover, but it must have been a riot to the lords and ladies who heard the story.

But even while we laugh, we can't forget that the young man left his poor old mother brokenhearted.

## A Change of Atmosphere

The beginning of this tale may give us a few more laughs than the average romance, but otherwise it is pretty much what we would expect: a battle here, a damsel there, and a handsome young hero who seems invincible. Messengers scurry to Arthur's court with news of the unknown young Welshman's feats of battle and valor.

Now it's time for his characteristic failure to do its dramatic work in pushing the plot forward.

Looking for a night's lodging, the young knight comes to the house of a noble lord, who gives him some good advice about being a knight:

> Be careful lest you talk too much
> Or waste your time with chat and such:
> Whoever wastes his breath that way
> Will say some things he shouldn't say.

We all know what happens when this fellow gets good advice, so we're all set for another laugh riot the next time he meets some poor unsuspecting damsel. But what we get is hardly what we expected.

It isn't long before the young man has a chance to misapply the advice he got. In his wanderings, the young knight stops to ask directions of a fisherman, and the fisherman offers to lodge him in his own house. You can imagine how surprised our hero is to discover, right where the fisherman said his house would be, a fine and beautiful castle, where the young knight is received with every honor and courtesy. Well, his host does omit one courtesy, but for that he has a good excuse:

> I do not stand up as I ought;
> Forgive me, sir, for I cannot.

The lord of the castle is lame, which in itself doesn't seem very unusual. But strange things begin to happen immediately.

First, a squire arrives with an almost supernaturally magnificent sword as a gift for the lord, and the lord turns it over to his guest. "Good sir, this was destined for you, and I desire you to have it."

Such generosity might seem unusual, but perhaps not extraordinary. What happens next, however, is so odd that we can only sit, like our hero, in open-jawed wonder.

> And while they spoke of sundry things,
> A young squire entered from the wings
> Holding a lance of brilliant white
> Grasped by the middle. In the light
> Of the warm fire as he passed by,
> They saw the white tip raised on high;
> And from it came a single drop
> Of blood that flowed down from the top,
> Which, running downward from the head,
> Stained the squire's hand vermilion red.

What on earth is going on here? We're in the dark, but does our hero ask the obvious question? No: he picks this moment to remember the very good advice he got about talking too much. He thinks it would be rude to ask even a simple question. What an annoying fellow he can be when he's got an idea stuck in his head! But the bleeding spear is only the beginning of the marvels.

> Then coming in by the same door,
> Two handsome squires marched in; each bore
> A candelabra, rich and fine,
> From each of which ten lights did shine.
> Then came a damsel, who did hold

A grail made of the finest gold
Between her hands. She walked with grace,
Beautifully dressed and fair of face;
And when she entered with the grail,
A light that made the candles pale
Shone out, as when the sun shines bright,
And makes the pale stars lose their light.
And after her, one damsel more
A platter made of silver bore.
The grail itself was made of gold,
And settings all around did hold
All sorts of precious stones, as rare
As any gems found anywhere
On land or sea, exceeding far
In worth all other stones there are.
And, just as with the lance before,
They went out through another door.

Here, surely, is a time when one might politely ask a
small question. But the young knight won't. He still sits
mute, remembering that wise advice he got. And we, the
audience, are about to tear out our hair in frustration. It
doesn't help that Chrétien can't forbear teasing us a little:

The young man watched them enter there,
But not a question did he dare
To ask, either about the grail
Or whom it served: he did not fail

To take his teacher's words to heart.
He did not speak, and for my part
I fear some harm might come of this,
For I've heard tell that one can miss
As much by silence as by speech.

This must be one of the most frustrating moments in the history of literature, and we can incidentally admire Chrétien's confidence that the "harm" he fears will not be directed at him by the audience.

After this strange parade, dinner is served, and—wouldn't you know it—that same grail passes by again, and our hero still keeps his mouth shut. Course after course is served, and each new course brings another grail sighting, and still the young man is silent. The best we get out of him is a mental note that he really must remember to ask one of the staff about the grail before he leaves the next morning.

But the next morning is too late. Our hero wakes at daybreak to find the castle deserted: no lord, no servants. And when the young knight leaves, the drawbridge closes by itself a little too quickly—the medieval equivalent of getting smacked by the swinging door on your way out.

Chrétien de Troyes's tale begins to look like something more than popular entertainment. It almost seems like allegory. In looking for the knightly life of chivalry, our lad seems to be stumbling on deeper mysteries.

In fact, he's discovering that what he hoped would give his life purpose will not make him complete after all.

Perhaps he was more right than we knew at the beginning of the story: he was looking at knights in armor, but he was really hoping for God and his angels.

## He Should Have Asked

We've just had our first encounter with what will become the Holy Grail in later stories, but so far we know next to nothing about it. Obviously it bears some importance, since it was paraded in front of the young knight's face so many times, as if his host was daring him to ask a question about it.

Now, the term *grail* held no mystery for Chrétien or his audience. It was an ordinary term for the sort of broad platter that might have been used to serve one of the fish or meat courses at a medieval feast.[1] The word was a bit unusual, perhaps, but no more mysterious than, say, *tureen* is to us. What was notable about this particular grail was, first, it was very richly decorated (but that in itself was not terribly surprising in view of the obvious wealth of the host); and, second, it was constantly paraded right by the guests with great pomp and ceremony and then whisked into a hidden room, without our hero even having the opportunity to see what was in it.

What was this grail? And who was to be served from this platter that passed through the hall without stopping? These are the questions we desperately wanted the young knight to ask, but he missed his chance.

On his way from the deserted castle, our young hero comes across a damsel mourning over the headless body of a knight. She turns out to be a remarkably useful acquaintance: she can explain several of the mysteries that have been puzzling our hero.

The fisherman and lord of the castle (they are one and the same) is the rich Fisher King. Wounded through both thighs by a javelin, he lives in constant pain, and fishing is the only diversion he can endure.

Having said so much, the damsel asks our hero whether he saw the bleeding lance. He answers in the affirmative. The damsel wants to know if he asked why the lance bled. When he says that he didn't, the damsel tells him he has done badly. Did he see the grail? Our hero describes the procession he saw but again admits that he asked no questions.

"As God may help me, that was worse," she declares.

Then she has one more question for him: what is his name?

Until now, the young man has never needed a name. But until now he has never been conscious of failure. Now, confronted with the overwhelming evidence that he has not succeeded in the adventure of the Fisher King's castle, he somehow guesses his name: Perceval of Wales.

But the words have hardly passed his lips when the damsel tells him that his name has changed—to Perceval the Miserable. She has more bad news for him: his mother has died of grief since he left her, and this damsel ought to know because she is his first cousin and saw his mother buried. She also tells him not to trust the fine-looking sword he got last night, for it will break in pieces when he needs it most.

Perceval certainly is miserable now. Until today, he has never doubted himself in any situation; now he knows that everything he has done so far has been a failure. He will fail in the future, too, if the damsel's prophecy is true. He doesn't even know what the purpose of his life is anymore. In short, Perceval has been torn down, and he will have to be rebuilt.

## The Misery on the Other Side

We, the audience, are about to feel the same way. In the beginning, we laughed at the antics of the young bumpkin who misinterpreted every piece of good advice he ever got. Now we meet one of the victims of that comedy, and suddenly it doesn't seem so funny. Because of Perceval's ignorance, an innocent young woman has been condemned to a life of intolerable misery by the mad jealousy of her lover. We laughed when he stole her ring and drowned her in amateurish kisses; now we see what the consequences were. It's a shock both to Perceval and to us, and it's a bit of a daredevil feat on Chrétien's part. Few writers have entertained so well with comedy and then dared to lift the curtain and show the misery on the other side.

This appears to be about as low as Perceval can get, and he now begins a slow and painful reform. At first, however, his reform seems to be only a matter of living up to the common expectations of a chivalrous knight. He starts by making amends for the wrongs he did to the innocent woman: he defeats her husband in battle and exacts a promise from him that he will wash and dress her properly, let her rest, and then take her to King Arthur's court and tell everyone the whole story. The man keeps his promise faithfully, and once again Arthur's court is astonished by news of the young Welshman's feats of arms. Arthur himself swears never to stay in the same place two nights in a row until he finds the young knight who has been doing him such good services.

It doesn't take long. The next morning, Arthur's knights find Perceval. Two knights try to bring him back by force and fail, with bruises and broken bones for their trouble; a courteous knight named Gawain tries friendliness and succeeds, and makes a permanent friend as well.

On the third day after Perceval's arrival at Arthur's court, the most appallingly hideous woman anyone has ever seen rides her mule straight into the presence of the king and launches a volley of accusations against Perceval. He failed to ask about the lance and the grail when he had the chance. If he had asked, the Fisher King would have been healed, and his land would have been at peace. Now war will ravage the land, all for the lack of a simple question.

But that's not the only news she brings. In a certain castle is a maiden besieged, and great will be the honor to any knight who can raise the siege and rescue the maiden.

Gawain vows at once that he will be the one to rescue the maiden. Perceval, meanwhile, swears never to stay in the same place two nights in a row until he learns who is served by the grail and why the lance is bleeding.

Here we, the modern readers who remember that this is the first Grail romance, are probably thinking that at last the quest for the Holy Grail has begun in earnest, and we might reasonably expect to follow Perceval's adventures until he finds it at last. Actually, that isn't what happens at all. This is the last we hear of Perceval for a long time. Instead, we follow the many adventures of Gawain.

## The Secret of the Grail

When we finally get back to Perceval, five years have gone by. Perceval is a wreck: he has forgotten himself so much that he has "forgotten God." This is the first outright admission we've had that his problems might have a spiritual dimension. Is Chrétien—the poet of courtly love—turning religious on us?

It begins to look that way. We could almost say that Perceval has reached the same low point that Chrétien's audience had already reached before he began his tale—perhaps the same point that Chrétien himself had reached when he wrote his story of the Knight of the Cart. In their mad pursuit of love, they had forgotten God so completely that they had turned sin into virtue.

We thought Perceval was low before, but now he's really hit rock bottom. He has no idea what's going on when he sees knights and ladies walking barefoot in penitential robes; he has to be told that it's Good Friday and that it's a shocking sin to appear in arms on Good Friday. He even has to be told who Jesus Christ is and what happened to him on Good Friday. Perhaps this is exactly what Chrétien's audience needed to hear as well.

A handy hermit, who also turns out to be Perceval's uncle, takes it from there.

Perceval knows now that his real problem is spiritual: he has forgotten God. His reform will also have to be spiritual.

The hermit agrees that the problem is spiritual. He explains that it is sin that has caused all of Perceval's problems: the unpardoned sin of causing his mother so much grief. Sin closed his mouth at the castle so that he failed to ask the question he ought to have asked. All the other sorrows Perceval has endured have been a result of the same sin.

The hermit also reveals the secret of the grail, or at least part of it: the grail serves none other than Perceval's other uncle, the father of the rich Fisher King, who stays in that back room where Perceval saw the grail procession go after it passed him. And the grail contains no ordinary food, but a single Mass wafer; the old king is so holy that he needs nothing else to sustain him. He has lived in that back room for fifteen years without coming out.

All this casts a new light on the story. We suddenly have a hint that perhaps the previous events had some sort of meaning beyond themselves. We thought Perceval was making his own mistakes; now we're being told that it was sin dwelling within him that caused him all this grief.

The remedy for sin is repentance and the sacrament of penance. Perceval will have to live a new kind of life. The hermit's advice to Perceval shows us what it means to live in a Eucharistic culture—what it means for a secular life to become holy:

- Repent.
- Go to church first thing every morning.
- Stay all the way through Mass.
- Love, believe, and worship God.
- Show respect to worthy men and women.
- Show respect to priests.
- Help widows, girls, and orphans.

The method is simple: make God and the Mass the center of your life, be humble, and help the helpless. Not easy, but simple. Perceval gladly accepts his penance. And then,

> the hermit taught him an orison and repeated it till he knew it by heart. In this prayer were many names of our Lord, and they were so great that

mouth of man ought not to utter them save in the fear of death. So after teaching the prayer, he forbade Perceval to say it except in great peril, and Perceval said: "Sir, I will not."

This is a striking incident. We want to know more about this secret and powerful prayer, and we're confident that it will come up again at some crucial point in the story. Chrétien, master craftsman that he was, would not have introduced this prayer if he had not intended to make use of it later.

## The Nature of True Worthiness

The result of Perceval's penance is worthiness—which perhaps is what he was really looking for all along, just like the warriors in the ancient story of the Cauldron of the Chieftain of Annwfn. With worthiness comes a consciousness of the truth of the Christian religion. "Thus Perceval came to recognize that God received death and was crucified on the Friday. And at Easter, most worthily, Perceval received communion."

We seem to have come a long way—and quickly, too—from the world of courtly love and casual adultery.

At this point in the story, Chrétien left Perceval in order to follow Gawain again. Before he was through with Gawain's adventures, Chrétien put down his pen.[2] Then he died, and his last—and possibly greatest—romance was left forever unfinished.

Or at least unfinished by Chrétien. By the time of his death, he was a literary superstar. An unfinished romance by the great Chrétien—especially one filled with mysteries to be unraveled—was too great a temptation for would-be successors to pass by.

*The Story of the Grail* had started out as a type of comedy of manners, but it led the lords and ladies who heard it into deeper waters than they had expected. There was something more meaningful in it than just a tale of knightly adventure. When the unfinished romance was read in court, more than one knight must have gone home a bit more pensive than usual, wondering if he might somehow be as lost in the woods as Perceval was. Perhaps there was something better than courtly love and colorful adventure. Perhaps the real goal was, after all, worthiness.

# ✝
# Chapter the Tenth

## Which Takes Us into the Shadowy Wood
## Where Allegories Lurk Unseen

UNFINISHED THOUGH IT WAS, CHRÉTIEN'S *Story of the Grail* was a literary sensation. But it left the whole literate world with one burning question: *then* what happened?

It was an irresistible puzzle. Several writers tried their hand at picking up where Chrétien left off, but they lurched wildly in different directions. Instead of trying to finish the story the way they thought Chrétien would have done it, they ended up using Chrétien's work as a relatively short prologue to their own ungainly and rambling compositions.

Like some strange literary snowball, the romance just kept rolling on, picking up more and more debris as it went. There were continuations, and continuations of the continuations. There were "prequels," too, to use a modern Hollywood term: a history of the Grail and how it became holy, and a story that explained how Perceval and his mother ended up hidden in the forest. In some manuscripts, a clumsy editor attempted to weld alternative continuations into one horribly confused narration. Chrétien's carefully constructed tale got buried somewhere in the middle of a vast wilderness of unlikely adventures.

## The Habit of Allegory

Still, a pattern does start to form in these meanderings. What really seems to have appealed to the next generation of writers was the suggestion that the adventures of Perceval were more than romantic pageantry, that they might also have some sort of allegorical significance.

It's foolish to talk glibly about "the medieval mind," as though the millions of people who lived during the Middle Ages shared a single mind and thought the same thoughts. But there were certain popular habits of thought, as there are now, that we can take as characteristic of the age.

One of those was the habit of seeing symbols and allegories in everything. Scripture could be interpreted symbolically and allegorically, yet it was an acknowledged fact that Scripture was also an accurate record of historical events. The allegorical interpretation was possible because the same God who was the author of Scripture was also the author of history, and of all creation as well.

But if that was true, then it was equally possible to interpret things other than Scripture in a symbolic sense. That's precisely what the medieval writers loved to do.

One of the most obvious examples of that sort of symbolic interpretation is the bestiary, or animal book. Herds of bestiaries have survived from the Middle Ages, and in them we can see, hard at work, the medieval quest for the allegorical meaning of things. These books, many of them richly illuminated, describe the nature and habits of the animals known—or thought to be known—to medieval Europeans.

But physical description is only part of each entry: the rest explains the allegorical lesson to be learned from each animal.

The lion, for example, rubs out its traces with its tail when hunters pursue it, so that the hunters lose the trail. The Aberdeen Bestiary gives us that supposed fact, then develops the allegory: "Even so our Savior, who is a spiritual lion, . . . hid the traces of his love in heaven, until, when he was sent by the Father, he descended into the womb of the Virgin Mary and saved the human race, which was lost."

The ibex has two horns so strong that they can support its weight when it is in danger of falling into an abyss. "This signifies the learned men who, with the harmony of the two testaments, can manage whatever difficulties come up."

However grand or lowly the creature—lion or weasel, elephant or worm—it had a meaning beyond itself. Every creature was the bearer of an allegorical message from the Creator, and the chief duty of medieval natural history was to decipher those messages.

Once Chrétien had brought up the idea, later writers found that the world of Arthur was the perfect environment for allegory. It was already a world where events had meanings beyond themselves. From Gildas on, the British had always interpreted that part of their story the way Old Testament writers interpreted the history of Israel. Defeats were God's judgment on the sins of the people; victories happened only when the people turned from their sins.

## The Snare of Heresy

As all these would-be successors to Chrétien groped their way toward a religious allegory, they neglected the one thing in Chrétien's story that we might have expected them to embrace most enthusiastically. In all the tens of thousands of lines they wrote, not one of them ever brought up that secret prayer Perceval learned from his uncle the hermit.

It seems like too good an opportunity to miss. Chrétien set it up very carefully; we know that Perceval could utter the prayer when he was in grave danger and be saved just in the nick of time. It is hardly possible that the other writers simply forgot about the hermit's prayer. Not only is it striking in itself, but it comes at the very end of the Perceval section. It is almost the last impression we get of Perceval in Chrétien's romance. Still, none of the other writers made anything of it. Why not?

The simple answer is that they were not heretics. We can only guess how Chrétien would have used the prayer, but regardless of how it is used, the prayer is heretical, because it derives its power from knowledge of the secret names of God. Such use of secret names of God, angels, and demons was all the rage during the Middle Ages, among magicians and occultists of both Jewish and Christian persuasion. The prayer taught to Perceval is not a prayer at all, but a magic spell. As later writers developed the religious implications of the story, they carefully ignored the hermit's prayer. That's a telling indication of how seriously they took their productions. They were willing to pass up an easy triumph, all wrapped up by Chrétien and ready to go, because it wouldn't pass their test of orthodoxy.

But does this mean that Chrétien was a heretic? Almost certainly not. To be a heretic requires willful defiance of the teachings of the church. Everything else in the hermit's advice is quite orthodox, including the commandments to go to church every day, stay all the way through the Mass, and show respect to priests—surely not the precepts of a deliberate heretic. There is not the least trace of anti-clericalism, let alone heresy.

Chrétien was a storyteller, not a theologian. Any storyteller can see that he was setting the stage for a miraculous deliverance. At some point later in the story,

Perceval would find himself in mortal peril. We would be on the edge of our seats, holding our breath, certain that our hero was about to die. And then, at the last possible moment, Perceval would remember the hermit's magic prayer, and the miraculous deliverance would follow immediately, and we would all be so delighted that we would stand up and cheer.

This is the storytelling triumph that Chrétien was no doubt imagining. The idea that his triumph would also be heresy probably did not occur to Chrétien. But it did occur to his successors. The remarkable fact that they all passed up such a marvelous storytelling opportunity shows us how deeply concerned they were with religious orthodoxy. It was not likely that a writer of romances would get into trouble for including a silly bit of magic in his story, but the writers of the Grail romances were more than romancers. They were developing a profound—and orthodox—religious allegory of the Eucharist.

## The Self-Interpreting Allegory

It's easy to get carried away with allegorical interpretations. "Certain modern commentators," says the famous Grail scholar Pauline Matarasso, "ignoring St. Bernard's advice to pass quickly through the shadowy wood where allegories lurk unseen, have become so bewitched by the chase that they have never reemerged on the open plain of moral truths."[1] The temptation is to see allegories everywhere and to give the simplest stories the most complicated and unlikeliest interpretations.

In light of this, it's worth pointing out that interpreting the Holy Grail stories allegorically is not getting carried away. We can say this with confidence because the authors themselves offer us allegorical interpretations of their stories. Whenever a strange thing happens to a knight, a hermit is always nearby to explain the hidden meaning of it. Chrétien himself gave us the first in this long line of handy hermits, and the romancers who followed knew a good trick when they saw one. Allegory is no good, after all, if no one gets the point. If their purpose had been merely to show off their skill to the literary elite, the writers might have taken their chances and left it to the reader to discover the hidden meanings in their tales. But their purpose was to change lives, and for that they needed to make sure their point got across.

There are, however, plenty of pitfalls on the winding path through St. Bernard's allegorical forest.

✝

# Chapter the Eleventh

## In Which the Unfinished Story of the Grail Tempts Many a Writer to Take Up His Pen

POWERFUL FORCES TEND TO PULL THE story of the Grail toward heresy—particularly toward Gnosticism. In the hands of a careless romancer, the Grail quest can turn into a quest for secret knowledge—that is, knowledge that God has deliberately withheld from the rabble and revealed only to an elite core of perfect believers.

We remember the old Celtic stories of cauldrons of knowledge, like the one that burned Taliesin's fingers. Secret knowledge has always had a powerful appeal. We need only walk into the self-help section of any bookstore to see that the appeal has not withered; just count the number of books with the word *secrets* right in the title. If only we, like Taliesin, had all the knowledge in the world, we'd know what it was we were longing for so desperately and how to go about getting it.

But if the Grail holds secret knowledge, what will that knowledge be? And if everybody in the audience learns the secret at the end of the romance, then it's not much of a secret anymore, is it?

## One Big Allegory

The French poet Robert de Boron, whose version of the Grail story, told in a trilogy of poems, had an important influence on later romancers, has Christ himself whispering secret teachings to Joseph of Arimathea—teachings so secret that Robert will not reveal them: "And I beg all those who hear this tale to ask me no more about it at this point, for I should have to lie."[1]

In Robert's version, this secret teaching is possessed by the keepers of the Grail. The Grail and the secret knowledge are passed down from Joseph and end up with the Fisher King. When Perceval, the best knight in the world, comes to the court of the maimed Fisher King and asks who is served by the Grail, the Fisher King will be whole again. "Then he will tell him the secret words of our Lord before passing from life to death." When Perceval finally achieves the Grail, he learns the secret teachings—but Robert still can't tell them to us.

This idea of a secret teaching of Jesus, revealed to only a few and concealed from most of the church, is the essence of Christian Gnosticism. That's not to say that Robert was a heretic. Once again, to be a heretic one must willfully defy the teachings of the church, and Robert almost certainly did not intend to promote heresy. Like Chrétien with his secret prayer, he was probably just carried away by his storytelling.

Robert de Boron is seldom read today, but he deserves to be remembered as the first writer to see the full potential of the Arthurian cycle. He was the first to imagine the whole story of King Arthur's court as one vast but integrated religious allegory, and he put the Holy Grail right at the center of it. His mind was not deep or subtle enough to carry out his daring plan with complete success. But the idea was his, and the later masterpieces of Arthurian romance owe their very being to him.

## The McGuffin

Chrétien wrote in rhymed verse, and Arthurian stories in verse were popular up through Tennyson and beyond. But a little while after Chrétien, the idea of writing romances in prose suddenly caught on. In essence, the medieval writers invented the novel.[2]

We could even say that the novel was invented to deal with the Holy Grail. Chrétien, as we said, wrote in verse, and so did the romancers who continued his *Story of the Grail*. Robert de Boron started writing his romances in verse and finished in prose. *The High Book of the Grail*, written by an anonymous author in the 1200s, is entirely in prose.

After that, almost all the Grail romances were written in prose. Arthurian romances in verse were still common, but none of them mentioned the Grail. An English verse romance called *Sir Perceval of Wales* even manages to give us the whole life of Perceval without hinting at the Grail at all.

The reason for this divergence is fairly simple. Verse was a form appropriate for popular entertainment; serious histories and treatises were written in prose. The story of the Holy Grail had passed from frivolous entertainment to serious moral instruction. And it seems almost too appropriate that the transition happened right in the middle of Robert de Boron's attempt at an allegorical romance.

One of the most famous Grail romances came from the pen of a delightfully eccentric Bavarian named Wolfram von Eschenbach. Wolfram's *Parzival,* a verse romance written in the early 1200s, stands entirely outside the mainstream of Grail romances. It's as eccentric as its author, whose strange combination of deep thought and playful wit shows through on every page. Though Wolfram's story roughly follows Chrétien's outline, the central mystery has been changed. In *Parzival,* the Grail is not a dish or a cup or a vessel of any sort. Instead, it's a magical gem with miraculous healing powers.[3]

Wolfram shows us how quickly the idea of the Grail as object of desire had taken hold, and how thoroughly the meaning of the word *grail* had changed. In Chrétien's time, it was a somewhat unusual term for a type of serving dish; the mystery lay in what the grail held and in the elaborate ceremony that surrounded it.

By the time Wolfram wrote his Grail romance, the word *grail* had come to stand for the mystery itself, the object of hope and desire—but the individual romancer was free to determine what object the Grail actually was. It had almost become what Alfred Hitchcock used to call a McGuffin: a thing that sets the plot going but whose exact nature isn't really important to the story.

The idea of the Grail as a magical gem never really caught on with other writers. Wolfram's romance was a big hit by medieval standards, and—as we'll see later—it would find some very surprising champions in the twentieth century. But it had little or no influence on the string of French romances that would develop the Grail story as we usually remember it.

## In the Name of the Father, and of the Son, and of the Holy Ghost

So far we've seen just the beginnings of allegory in the Arthurian romances. The stories are still, in the main, stories: the allegory seems to be an interpretation layered on afterward.

But not long after Robert de Boron, another writer, who remained anonymous, picked up his pen to turn all the conventions of Arthurian romance upside down. "The High Book of the Grail begins in the name of the Father, and of the Son, and of the Holy Ghost," he wrote, and then he began to set a scene that seems completely foreign to Arthurian romance. In this story, Arthur is no longer the best king in the world, but the worst. By lethargy, he has fallen from his exalted moral position, and it will take some serious work for him to get back where he belongs.

At once we are plunged into a world where the line between dreaming and waking has been obliterated. The history begins with the terrifying tale of a squire who dreams that he takes a golden candlestick from a chapel and is stabbed for his crime by a big ugly stranger. Though he has never really left King Arthur's hall, he wakes mortally wounded, with the knife in his side and the candlestick stuffed into his hose, where he had put it in his dream.

We have been warned: the dreamworld has erupted into waking life with deadly force, and from now on waking life will follow the logic of a dream. We're back in the hazy world of Celtic legend, where the Otherworld might burst in on us at any moment.

Dreams bring abstract ideas to life in symbolic form, and that is what happens in *The High Book of the Grail*. In earlier romances, the events could have allegorical significance; that is, they could illustrate abstract ideas. But now the events *are* abstract ideas come to concrete life; they happen only because they ought to happen. The symbolic cause alone is enough to set events in motion—there is no need for any physical cause. *Every* event in the story has an allegorical meaning.

Here is something new and good, and it's obvious that a completely different purpose drove the creator to write this romance. Chrétien and Robert were storytellers who added allegorical layers to their tales, but this new writer is a theologian and moralist who writes a story specifically to convey moral and theological truth. The truth is what drives the story.

The weakness of this method is that it tends to divorce the story from reality. The dreamlike images and weird adventures keep us listening to the story, but the world of the romance is too different from our own to make a big dent in our sense of self. We can watch Arthur search for redemption without seriously wishing we were searching with him; we can see Perceval achieve the Grail without seriously hoping that we might one day be as worthy as Perceval is. The characters in the story feel an insatiable longing for worthiness and holiness, but the feeling doesn't easily make the leap from the story to the audience. As an entertainment, and even as an intellectual exercise, *The High Book of the Grail* is a success; as a call to conversion, it's something of a failure.

But at the time, a book like this was needed. On the one side, the Albigenses—who threatened to overwhelm southern France with their neo-Gnostic heresy—were denying the power of the Eucharist. On the other side, the disciples of Ovid were making graven images to love. The Albigenses preached that the body was evil; the Ovidians lived for nothing but the body. Orthodox Christianity was actually in serious danger, especially among the upper classes.

What the age really needed was a romance that felt true to life, in which all the action sprang from believable human causes, but in which every event nevertheless had its symbolic and moral significance. The world of the romance needed to be close enough to the world of the medieval court that the lords and ladies who heard the story could see themselves in it. They would feel the insatiable longing that the heroes in the story felt, and they would come to recognize it for what it was: a longing for worthiness, for holiness, for communion with God.

A romance like that would be a tricky balancing act—one that would be far beyond the powers of most poets or novelists of any age.

✝

# Chapter the Twelfth

## In Which the Mysterious Master Walter Map Begins to Weave a Grand Allegory of Sin and Redemption

I MAGINE JUST FOR A MOMENT THAT medieval literary patrons are like television network executives (which might not be such a far-fetched analogy after all), and that we have to "pitch" a new romance to a patron the way would-be producers pitch a new television series. How can we convince our patron that we've got a surefire hit?

First, we need a big star. So we'll pick Lancelot, the most gallant knight there ever was, every lady's favorite and every lord's model. How can we go wrong with him?

Now we need a subject—or rather several subjects, since a romance, like a television series, can spread out over weeks or months of telling. First, we'll promise our patron a full account of the love of Lancelot and Guinevere; that alone practically guarantees success. Next, we'll include the real story of the Holy Grail, with all its mysteries revealed. That will grab the attention of the people who would read supermarket tabloids if there were any supermarket tabloids.

Finally, we can assure our patron that we'll have more dazzling pageantry, more tantalizing mystery, more intense love scenes, more heart-wrenching tragedy, more thrilling adventures, more epic sweep than any romance yet produced.

If that doesn't get him, he's just dead. We've come up with a formula for the perfect romance, and we're sure our patron will be drooling with anticipation.

We don't have to mention to him that our romance will also be a subversive time bomb that could destroy his whole way of life. There's no need to bother him with details.

## Who Is Walter Map?

The greatest of all the Arthurian romances was written by Walter Map. Or, more likely, it wasn't. The mystery of Walter Map is almost as fascinating to scholars as the mystery of Arthur himself. Yet again, an Arthurian text presents us with the sort of problem that can earn generations of scholars their doctorates.

We call the author of this gigantic epic Walter Map, because the text itself tells us that Master Walter Map wrote it. When we get such a clear identification of an author from a medieval romance, it seems a pity to spoil it with further speculation.

Nevertheless, there is very good reason to suppose that the five sections of the cycle were written by different people, not one of whom was Walter Map. The theory of a single author, the best scholars say, cannot account for the marked differences in style and vocabulary among the sections.

On the other hand, the theory of separate authors cannot account for the obvious unity of the sections. The first part constantly foreshadows events that will come to pass in the later parts, and the later parts constantly refer back to the earlier parts. Each part is painfully incomplete without the others.

We're left with a paradox: the cycle can't possibly be by one author, and it can't possibly be by more than one.

To get around this difficulty, some modern scholars have adopted a theory that barely seems plausible: one man acted as "architect" of the whole cycle and possibly wrote one part himself, but he farmed out subsequent sections to writers who could be trusted to carry out his plan. This theory asks us to believe in a sort of romance "studio" that operated in much the same way as a television network today. The only defense for the theory is that it accounts for some very unaccountable facts.

It may be that a sort of creative team was necessary for a project of its size. The cycle is enormous. Just scribbling so many words would have been a heroic labor.

We may have another clue as to the nature of the Walter Map romance studio. The twentieth-century historian Etienne Gilson argued pretty convincingly that Cistercian theology is behind *The Quest of the Holy Grail,* one of the sections of the cycle. Is it possible that some group in a certain Cistercian house undertook this giant novel as a holy work? It is another wild speculation, but monastic discipline would go a long way toward explaining how multiple authors with demonstrably different styles could produce such an obviously unified work.

An alternative theory suggests that the "architect" of the cycle took over an already existing Lancelot romance and made it the first part of the cycle, carefully editing it and adding the foreshadowing of events to come in the later parts. This theory still leaves us with at least two authors for the latter parts of the cycle, but at least it reduces the size of the team.

Was the "architect" Walter Map? The only Walter Map known to history died around 1209, before the romances were written, if we are to believe the best modern scholarship. It is unlikely, scholars say, that any Walter Map actually had anything to do with writing these romances.

Still, the romances are attributed to Walter Map in the texts themselves. Medievalists know this gigantic opus by a number of awkward names: the Lancelot-Grail Cycle, the Vulgate Cycle, or the Pseudo-Map Cycle. Having acknowledged the strange mystery of its authorship, we'll continue to call the author "Walter Map," but always keeping in mind that "Walter Map" is probably a name like "Mark Twain" or "George Eliot"—a pseudonym that hides some author or series of authors who, in this case, will never be identified.

## The Master Craftsman

Whoever he was, or however many people he was, Walter Map was a master architect. Every incident, every character, and almost every phrase in his work functions on a narrative level and on a symbolic level. *The Quest of the Holy Grail,* the centerpiece of the great romantic cycle, is so carefully worked out that, as Etienne Gilson remarked, "we should hardly undertake to find ten lines together in it written for the mere pleasure of storytelling."

Gilson took the romances of Walter Map as evidence that medieval schools must have been full of sophisticated thinking (in opposition to Gaston Paris—inventor of the term *courtly love*—who had said that the Middle Ages had no philosophy). "When there is so much philosophy in an age's romances," Gilson argued, "it is hardly likely that there was none at all in its schools and universities."[1]

We might think that such a meticulous and sophisticated work would not be much fun to hear. But it is quite the reverse: Walter Map created the most exciting and memorable of all the medieval romances. Most of what we see of the Arthurian world in modern literature goes back to Walter Map.

Medieval romances were written mostly for a courtly audience: people who expected to be entertained with tales of adventure and love happening to people not too different from themselves. The tales of Chrétien perfectly fulfilled their expectations.

Walter Map's great romance would also fulfill their expectations—even better than Chrétien's did. The knights and ladies who heard it would be entertained indeed. Their hearts would beat faster at the battles; they would cheer for the victories and weep over the tragic defeats. They would wonder at the marvels and gasp at the glorious mysteries. They would never even notice that they were being led away from heresy and sin and toward truth and virtue.

It was Walter Map who solved the problem that had stumped the author of *The High Book of the Grail:* how to make a romance completely allegorical without losing its grounding in the real world that medieval lords and ladies knew—a romance that would draw in its audience so thoroughly that they would feel themselves longing for the true holiness that makes us worthy to meet the Grail.

He did it by plunging right into the world of courtly love. He would meet Ovid on Ovid's own turf.

✝

# Chapter the Thirteenth

## The Genesis of Lancelot; or, The History of a Perfect Worldly Knight

WALTER MAP'S FIRST BIG INNOVATION WAS to make Lancelot the focus of the whole Arthurian world. Lancelot is fallen man: created good, he falls by sin and destroys the paradise of Camelot. Yet he has in him that inborn longing for paradise, that certainty that there is something better than our world of sin and death.

With Lancelot at the center, the whole story of the Round Table becomes a giant allegory of sin and redemption—a story of the spiritual progress not just of a man but of humanity.

At first glance, Lancelot seems an odd choice for a Christian hero. In fact, he seems to be firmly on the side of Ovid, not of Christ.

But that's the subversive genius of Walter Map. All the disciples of Ovid look to Lancelot as their model. They'll follow him wherever he goes; in everything he does they see themselves. Now Lancelot himself will lead them away from Ovid and back to Christ.

## Sir Uzzah

In its basic form, the Walter Map cycle is made up of three romances, although two long introductory romances later brought the total to five.

The first of the three original parts begins with the genesis of Lancelot. His purpose in life is clearly stated: he is to defend the church and the helpless. But as soon as he reaches Arthur's court, he sees Guinevere and falls helplessly in love with her. After that, we follow Lancelot on a long series of adventures in which he builds up a reputation as the best knight in the world. Yet there are some things he can't do. Unlike the other Lancelot romances, in which Lancelot sometimes seems super-human, this one gives us a Lancelot who sometimes fails at a task. And when he does, a holy man is usually conveniently nearby to explain to him that his failure comes from some hidden sin. Lancelot knows very well what that sin is.

The way holiness works will be shown most clearly in Lancelot's closest encounter with the Holy Grail. An ancient priest is saying Mass over the Grail, and at the elevation, Lancelot sees what seems to be the figure of a full-grown man in the priest's arms. The aged priest is tottering under the weight; alarmed, Lancelot leans forward to steady the priest—and is instantly blasted by divine fire.

Part of this scene is familiar from all the medieval paintings of the Mass of St. Gregory. But Lancelot's actions, and the consequences, remind us of a scene from the Old Testament—an incident that happened as King David was bringing the Ark of the Covenant to his new capital of Jerusalem.

> They carried the ark of God on a new cart, and brought it out of the house of Abinadab, which was on the hill. Uzzah and Ahio, the sons of Abinadab, were driving the new cart. . . .
>
> When they came to the threshing floor of Nacon, Uzzah reached out his hand to the ark of God and took hold of it, for the oxen shook it. The anger of the LORD was kindled against Uzzah; and God struck him there because he reached out his hand to the ark; and he died there beside the ark of God. (2 Samuel 6:3, 6–7)

The resemblance between Lancelot and the biblical Uzzah is too close to be coincidence. A holy thing seems to be tottering; a man with the best intentions reaches out to help; God instantly strikes him down. Unworthy people cannot approach what is holy: holiness repels them. Lancelot, unlike Uzzah, does not die. Instead, he lies sick for twenty-four days—one for each of the twenty-four years of his adultery with the queen. He has been given a chance to repent.

These uncharacteristic defeats teach Lancelot a disturbing truth about himself. He may be the ideal worldly knight, but he cannot approach what is holy. Holiness rejects him.

## Deadly Holiness

Holiness is a deadly force: this is something that's made very clear in Scripture. It's especially important to remember this truth when we look at the Grail stories, because the Grail itself carries not only blessing but also condemnation. This can be difficult to understand. Even Pauline Matarasso, who probably knows more about Walter Map's quest than anyone else alive, seems baffled by that property of the Grail:

> Thus at the very heart of the Grail legend there lies a grave ambivalence in that the relics of the Last Supper and the Passion are made to appear responsible for the malefic enchantments and perils afflicting King Arthur's kingdom.[1]

To Matarasso and many other commentators, the only explanation for the "ambivalence" is that Walter Map wasn't sure of what to do with the fragments of Celtic myth he had to work with as the basis of his story. He needed to keep the basic outline of the Grail story that his audience was expecting, but it left him with an awkward gap in his allegory.

We might, however, remember that passage in Paul's first letter to the Corinthians, in which he warns people not to partake of the Eucharist unworthily:

> For this reason many of you are weak and ill, and some have died. But if we judged ourselves, we would not be judged. But when we are judged by the Lord, we are disciplined so that we may not be condemned along with the world. (1 Corinthians 11:30–32)

We remember that the cup of blessing may also be a cup of condemnation. This is not a contradiction, but rather an important truth about the nature of sin and the nature of holiness.

## Two Sides of the Same Coin

Although the idea of the Eucharist as judgment for the unworthy can be hard to grasp, it was something medieval Christians were almost too conscious of: as we've mentioned, most lay believers received the Sacrament no more than once a year. Today we sweep the notion of judgment under the rug so thoroughly that we are apt to see a fundamental contradiction at the heart of the Grail legend: the Holy Grail, the fountain of God's blessing and the object of our holiest quest, is also a plague on the land.

The medieval audience, however, would see no contradiction, but only a simple truth about the nature of holiness. When the land is full of sin, then *of course* the Holy Grail brings judgment. Only to the worthy does it bring blessing.

Now we can see that Walter Map's version of the Grail legend, far from being marred by surviving Celtic myths, transformed them into a lively illustration of orthodox Pauline theology.

Nor is it only the Grail that works this way. Throughout the Grail story, we see adventures that follow the same pattern: an object brings blessing to the worthy and condemnation to the unworthy. We'll see this in the Holy Grail itself, in the Siege (or "Seat") Perilous, in Galahad's shield, in Galahad's sword—in every case, the unworthy approach at their peril, but the worthy gain rich blessings.

It is certainly true that this pattern comes from the world of Celtic mythology, with its magical cauldrons that will not boil the food of a coward, and so on. But Christian storytellers have taken the arbitrary and unpredictable images of Celtic myths and made them operate according to strict Christian ethics.

All creation follows the same principle. The universe was paradise to Adam and Eve, but their sin changed it into a world full of curses. And this is the truth that the story of the Grail illustrates: God created blessings, but it is our own sin and unworthiness that turns them into curses.

In fact, Paul's warnings seem a bit mild when compared to some of the stories in the Old Testament. "For the LORD your God is a devouring fire," Moses warned his people—and the Israelites knew that he was speaking the literal truth (Deuteronomy 4:24).

When Aaron's sons made the wrong kind of offering to God, "fire came out from the presence of the LORD and consumed them" (Leviticus 10:2).

When the ungrateful Israelites complained about being stuck out in the desert, "the fire of the LORD burned against them, and consumed some outlying parts of the camp" (Numbers 11:1).

Holiness cannot be approached by the unworthy, even when the unworthy have good intentions.

Still, on the whole, Lancelot's career looks like one success after another. He has more earthly glory than any other knight, and he has the love of the most beautiful woman in the kingdom. He is as close to perfect as a knight can get—at least by worldly standards. But there is another set of standards, a severer one, by which he will be judged.

$+$

# Chapter the Fourteenth

The Entrance of Galahad; or, The History of a
Perfect Spiritual Knight

BY THE END OF THE FIRST part of Walter Map's
romance cycle, Lancelot, in spite of his occasional
failures, has developed a reputation as the best
knight in the world. Now comes the keystone of the great
romantic arch: the romance of the Holy Grail. Here we'll
learn just how much Lancelot's reputation is worth.

## An Invitation

Once again, the romance begins with Lancelot, and specifically with the sudden entrance of a beautiful woman
on horseback.

> On the eve of Pentecost, when the companions of
> the Round Table had come to Camelot and had
> heard Mass, and when the tables were about to be
> set at the noon hour, there entered the hall a very

fair damsel on horseback. It was evident that she had come in great haste, for her horse was still all in a sweat. Dismounting, she came before the king and saluted him with God's blessing.

"Sire," said she, "for God's sake, tell me if Lancelot is here."

"Yes, truly," the king replied, "see him yonder." And he pointed him out to her.

Then going directly up to him, she said: "Lancelot, in the name of King Pelles, I bid you to accompany me into the forest."

And he asked her in whose service she was.

"I belong," she said, "to him whose name I have just mentioned."

"And what is your need of me?" he inquired.

"That you shall soon see," she replied.

"Then in God's name," he said, "I will gladly go."[1]

This is the Lancelot we've come to expect: always ready to gallop after a beautiful woman who seems to need his help. But the task she has for him is not the sort of thing Lancelot has come to expect at all. He follows her, not to a besieged castle, but to a nunnery. There he finds that his two cousins Bors and Lyonel, also famous knights of the Round Table, are already guests. Naturally they're curious to know what brings him there; he tells them about the odd incident with the damsel on horseback.

And while they were conversing thus, three nuns came in bringing Galahad, so fair and shapely a youth that one could hardly find his equal in the world. Then she who was most highborn, gently weeping, took him by the hand, and standing before Lancelot, she said to him: "Sire, here I bring you our ward, our greatest joy, our comfort and our hope, that you may make him a knight. For to our thinking there is no more honorable man than you from whom he could receive the order of chivalry."

He looked at the youth and saw him to be so marvelously endowed with every beauty that he thought he would never again see such a fine figure of a man. And from the modesty which he saw in him he hoped for so much that he was greatly pleased to make him a knight.

So he replied to the ladies that he would not fail to perform this request, and that he would gladly make him a knight, since they wished it so.

"Sire," said she who had brought him in, "we wish it to be done tonight or tomorrow."

"In God's name," said he, "it shall be as you desire."

Some etymologists trace the name Galahad to the scriptural Gilead ("Galaad" in the Latin Bible)—a name translated as "heap of testimony," and famous for its balm, interpreted by medieval commentators as an Old Testament foreshadowing of Christ (see Jeremiah 8:22). Quite a suggestive name.

## Son of Lancelot

There's another interesting and familiar thing about this Galahad. Lancelot doesn't remark on it, but his cousins do: in addition to being "a fine figure of a man," Galahad also bears a striking resemblance to Lancelot. The resemblance is not a coincidence. Galahad, as we'll find out, is Lancelot's son. His mother was the virgin who carried the Grail in the procession that Lancelot saw years before.

In the romances, the bearer of the Grail is always a virgin, chaste and pure. Many medievalists have pointed out that a communion chalice was never properly carried by a female and have suggested that some form of heresy must lurk behind the description of the Grail procession. But in the most orthodox theology, it is admitted that one woman did bear the body and blood of Christ: the Virgin Mary, chaste and pure. The virgin in the Grail procession represents Mary. Furthermore, the Grail maiden would give birth to Galahad, who represents Christ.

At the same time, our author is careful to make it clear that the identification of Galahad with Christ and of his mother with Mary is incomplete. After she conceived Galahad by Lancelot, the maiden was no longer a virgin. She was replaced in the Grail procession by her still-pure cousin. Galahad is not actually Christ; rather, he will be the pattern of how a Christian can become identified with Christ by imitating Christ's example.

After he is made a knight, Galahad does not follow Lancelot back to Camelot; instead, he awaits the proper moment to make a dramatic appearance at King Arthur's court.

## A Sword in a Stone

Having knighted young Galahad, Lancelot returns in plenty of time for the Feast of Pentecost. Now, at the Round Table every knight had his own seat with his name engraved on it. But there was one empty seat, the Siege Perilous, in which no one dared sit. Those who were foolish enough to try it always suffered painful or fatal consequences. But today a fresh inscription appears on the Seat Perilous:

> FOUR HUNDRED AND FIFTY-FOUR YEARS ARE ACCOMPLISHED SINCE THE PASSION OF JESUS CHRIST; AND ON THE DAY OF PENTECOST THIS SEAT IS TO FIND ITS OCCUPANT.

This is a strange thing: according to the inscription, the Seat Perilous is to be occupied this very day.

Arthur and his companions are almost ready to sit down and eat when Kay, one of Arthur's knights, reminds them of the king's curious custom: he never sits down to eat on a high feast day until some notable adventure has come to pass. (Apparently the new inscription on the Seat Perilous isn't notable enough.)

Notable adventures are common in these parts. There's no time for stomachs to grumble in protest; immediately a breathless page enters the hall with the astonishing news that a huge red stone is floating on the water. By the time everyone reaches the water's edge, the stone has come to rest on the shore, and a beautiful sword is embedded in it.

You may remember the story of the sword that Arthur pulled out of the stone, the sword that proved him king of Britain. This is a different sword in a different stone, but it has some of the same properties. Like that other sword, this one rewards the worthy. It also punishes the unworthy, as we'll find out. The sword bears an inscription:

> NO ONE SHALL REMOVE ME FROM HERE BUT THE ONE AT WHOSE SIDE I AM DESTINED TO HANG. AND HE SHALL BE THE BEST KNIGHT IN THE WORLD.

The king immediately asks Lancelot to take the sword, since everyone knows that Lancelot is the best knight in the world. But here Lancelot is suddenly overcome by uncharacteristic self-doubt.

> "Surely, sire, neither is it mine, nor would I be so bold or so imprudent as to set my hand to it; for I

am neither sufficiently worthy nor adequate that I should take it. So I shall hold back and not touch it, for it would be madness on my part to seek to take it."

"But try anyhow, and see if you can pull it out."

"I will not, sire," said he, "for I know full well that if anyone tries and fails, he will receive a wound from it."

"And how do you know that?" the king inquired.

"Sire," he replied, "I know it well enough. And I will tell you still another thing; for I want you to know that this very day will begin the great adventures and marvels of the Holy Grail."

Something has pricked Lancelot's conscience, and it has something to do with the Holy Grail. Surprised, Arthur asks his nephew Gawain to try removing the sword. He tries, though unwillingly, and after him Perceval. Neither can budge it, and no more knights are willing to try.

## The Seat of Galahad

Kay points out that this certainly qualifies as a notable adventure, so they can all go back and eat. They do, and it is at this moment that Galahad makes his dramatic appearance. The windows of the palace close by themselves, and yet the hall is as bright as ever. Then a holy man enters the room, leading Galahad. "King Arthur, I bring thee the

Knight Desired, who is sprung from the high lineage of King David and from the family of Joseph of Arimathea; it is he through whom the marvels of this country and of foreign lands will terminate. Behold him here!"

It turns out that Galahad is the one for whom the sword was destined, and he was so confident of obtaining the sword that he came to Camelot without a sword of his own. And the Seat Perilous is destined for him, too: in place of the first inscription is a new one that simply reads,

THIS IS THE SEAT OF GALAHAD.

Here is another object that rewards the worthy and punishes the unworthy—just as the cauldrons and swords and cloaks in ancient Celtic legend did.

Obviously, this new young knight has some sort of glorious destiny ahead of him. All the signs point to it. But what will it be?

✝

# Chapter the Fifteenth

## In Which a Rash Vow Begins a Quest for the Deep Secrets and Confidences of Our Lord

ARTHUR'S PENTECOST HAS ALREADY BEEN notable for its adventures. But the adventures are about to become a good bit more notable.

Pentecost is a great feast at Arthur's court, and the way to celebrate a great feast at Camelot is with a tournament. Here Galahad proves himself as valiant a knight as ever sat at the Round Table. Then, before supper, everyone naturally goes to Mass. That's one thing Arthur's court never neglects.

### The Grail Feast

Having gone to Pentecost Mass, the knights come back to Arthur's hall for a great feast.

And when the king had come out from the church
and had come into the upper hall, he ordered the
tables to be laid. Then the knights went to take
their seats as they had done in the morning.

When they were all seated in silence, there was
heard such a great and marvelous peal of thunder
that it seemed to them the palace must collapse.
But at once there shone in upon them a ray of
sunlight which made the palace sevenfold brighter
than it was before. And straightway they were as
if illumined with the grace of the Holy Spirit, and
they began to look at one another; for they knew
not whence this experience had befallen them. Yet,
there was no man present who could speak or utter
a word: for great and small alike were dumb.

Then when they had remained for some time
so that none of them had power to speak, but
rather they gazed at each other like dumb beasts,
there entered the Holy Grail covered with a white
cloth; but no one was able to see who was carrying
it. It entered by the great door of the hall, and as
soon as it had come in, the hall was filled with
odors as sweet as if all the spices of the earth were
diffused there. And it passed down the middle of
the hall and all around the high seats; and as it
passed before the tables, they were straightway
filled at each place with such viands [food] as the
occupant desired.

When all were served, the Holy Grail departed at once so that they knew not what had become of it nor did they see which way it went.

At once the power of speech was restored to those who before could not utter a word. And most of them gave thanks to our Lord for the great honor he had done them in feeding them with the grace from the Holy Vessel. But more than all the others present, King Arthur was joyous and glad because our Lord had shown him greater favor than to any king before him.

The Holy Grail offers its gifts indiscriminately to all the knights of the Round Table. The grace of the Holy Spirit comes freely to everyone; the seed is scattered over every kind of ground. But only a few can respond to the call. All the others sprout and wither.

## Pentecost Parallels

The first apparition of the Grail deliberately parallels the story of Pentecost in the New Testament book of Acts, chapter 2.

- It happens on the day of Pentecost.

- There is a sound of thunder ("the rush of a violent wind" in the New Revised Standard Version).

- All the principal characters are gathered in one room.

- They are "illumined with the grace of the Holy Spirit."

But there is also a noteworthy difference: at Pentecost, the apostles were given the gift of languages, so that all the people who had gathered in Jerusalem from the farthest corners of the earth heard them preaching in their own languages. The companions of the Round Table, however, are struck completely dumb. They are unholy men in the presence of holiness.

And there is an interesting addition. The Holy Grail serves each one the food he most desires. This comes not from Scripture, but straight from the misty depths of Celtic legend.

Thus the familiars and the strangers at the court alike rejoiced, for it seemed to them that our Lord had not forgotten them in showing them such a favor. And they continued to speak of it as long as the meal lasted. The king himself spoke of it to those who were seated nearest to him, and said: "Surely, my lords, we ought to be glad and rejoice greatly that our Lord has given such evidence of his love that he has consented to feed us with his grace upon such a high festival as Pentecost."

"Sire," replied my lord Gawain, "there is something else that you do not know: there is not a man here who has not been served with what he desired in his mind. And that is something that never happened in any court, unless it be in that of the Cripple King. But they are all so confounded that they could not see it openly, the true likeness being concealed from them. Wherefore, for my part I make this vow, to enter tomorrow without delay upon the quest and to prosecute it for a year and a day, and longer yet if need be; and I will not return to court for any reason whatsoever until I have seen it more clearly than it has been manifested to me here, if peradventure it be destined that I can behold it. And if it be destined otherwise, I will return."

When the knights of the Round Table heard these words, they all rose from their seats and made the same vow that my lord Gawain had made, and said they would not cease from their wandering until they should have sat at the high table where such sweet meat was daily served as that which they had just tasted.

And when the king saw that they had made this vow, he was in sore distress; for he knew well that he could not turn them aside from this enterprise. So he said to my lord Gawain: "Alas, Gawain, this vow which you have made will be the death of me,

for you have deprived me of the fairest and most
loyal company that I have ever found: the company
of the Round Table. For when they shall have left
me, whenever the time may come, I know well that
they will never all come back; rather will most of
them continue in this quest which will not end so
soon as you think."

This is an ominous prophecy, and ominous prophecies in romances nearly always come true. King Arthur
has built up "the fairest and most loyal company" of
knights ever seen in one place. His kingdom is the glory
of the ages, one that we happen to know will be held up
as a paragon of earthly glory in centuries to come. Yet the
quest for the Holy Grail will destroy this earthly kingdom—that, in effect, is what Arthur is saying, and he's
probably right.

## Much Earthly Worship

Still, the general opinion among the knights seems to be
that the quest is going to be a happy and colorful adventure, one that will win many a knight earthly glory and
the admiration of all the ladies. But then a wandering
holy man makes a dramatic entrance to spoil the fun.

Hear ye, lords of the Round Table who have sworn
to enter upon the quest of the Holy Grail! Nascien
the hermit sends you word by me that no one

shall take with him upon this quest either lady or damsel lest he fall into mortal sin: let no one enter upon it who is not confessed or who will not go to confession, for no one ought to enter upon such a lofty service before being cleansed and purged of all villainy and mortal sins. This quest is not a quest for earthly things, but is to be the search for the deep secrets and confidences of our Lord and for the great mysteries which the High Master will show openly to that fortunate knight whom he has elected among all the other knights of earth to be his servant. To him he will reveal the great marvel of the Holy Grail and will show him what mortal heart could not conceive nor the tongue of earthly man utter.

This certainly comes as a bit of a disappointment to the many brave knights who swore themselves to the quest in the heat of the moment. They expected "much earthly worship" from the quest, but it didn't occur to them that they would have to give up their lives of luxury and occasional debauchery. Wasn't impressing the damsels the reason they became knights in the first place?

Now they have to leave all that fun behind. Even more difficult, perhaps, is that they have to go to confession—where they'll have to confess all their adulteries and sincerely promise not to sin again if they want the absolution the wandering holy man says they need.

Still, the knights swore an oath, and no one would dare go back on that now. The ladies would never forgive them if they did.

Here, incidentally, we see the genius of Walter Map at work. Like *The High Book of the Grail,* this is a romance in which every incident has allegorical significance. But the story is artfully arranged so that every event also springs from very human motivations. It is, in other words, an exact reflection of real life, as real life would have been seen by a medieval thinker. Every knight in the audience would know how embarrassing it would be to go back on an oath like that, no matter how rashly taken. The psychology is perfectly sound; the motivations are perfectly plausible. Events in the world of Walter Map spring from worldly causes, but at the same time they follow God's providential plan. In a small way, Walter Map creates his allegory the same way God creates the whole universe.

This is the great turning point in Walter Map's long story. Up to now, we have seen Lancelot built up as the paragon of chivalry. Now it's time to shake his foundations. The whole world of chivalry—and perhaps our own ideas of earthly glory as well—will tremble and finally crash to the ground.

✝

# Chapter the Sixteenth

## The World Turned Upside Down

NOW WE'RE BEGINNING TO SEE WHY the great Lancelot-Grail Cycle was a subversive time bomb. The whole system of knightly ideals that governed court life was under attack. In the end, the true knight would not be the one who seduced the most beautiful women and won the most prestigious tournaments. The true knight would be the perfect servant of Jesus Christ.

Lancelot—the embodiment of all that was splendid in knighthood—would have to learn that his goals were the wrong goals. They had not satisfied his deepest longing. He would have to change his outlook completely; he would have to pursue not earthly glory but heavenly humility. He would have to make himself holy to meet the Holy Grail.

## Secular and Sacred

The thing that sets romances apart from most other medieval writings is that they are secular: they are not written by clerics for a mainly clerical audience. But many modern writers mistakenly suppose that "secular" is opposed to "sacred"—that what is "sacred" is confined to the church and has nothing to do with our ordinary lives.

Because modern students of the romances believe that sacred and secular must be opposites, they are puzzled when a secular romance runs into sacred territory. What are we to make of this burst of religion outside the church? "How," asks medieval scholar Richard Barber, "can medieval romances apparently invade the province of medieval religion, and how can secular authors write about the highest mysteries of the church?"[1]

If it is not officially sponsored by the church but involves itself in the business of religion, it must be heresy—this is the conclusion of many modern interpreters, who go on to applaud the courage of the heretical romancers in risking the flames of the Inquisition. Some trace the Grail romances to the Albigensian heresy—a notion that would shock and disgust the Albigenses, who would have found very little to their taste in the Arthurian romances. Many moderns dwell on the fact that "the medieval church never officially recognized the Grail stories,"[2] which is perfectly true, since the medieval church never "recognized" romances at all, any more than the modern church has "recognized" television shows or movies.

The difficulty disappears when we realize that sacred and secular are not opposites at all. Secular is the opposite of clerical, but a secular life can be, and for any Christian ought to be, sacred. The lay believer is called to holiness as much as a priest or a bishop or a monk. Walter Map is writing to show us exactly what it means for a secular life to be sacred. Lancelot's secular life until now has been nothing but sin; he must give up everything he has treasured if he is to make himself holy and worthy to achieve the Grail.

## The Wicked and Disloyal Servant

Lancelot is not the only paragon of chivalry who has to be torn down. All the popular heroes of Arthurian legend have to learn that their previous lives have been worthless—all flowers and no fruit. Since they left Arthur's court to pursue the Grail, most of them have had dreadfully humbling experiences.

Gawain, for example, has been trying to catch up with Galahad, and while on the road he is attacked by seven wicked knights whom Galahad has already defeated once. These knights captured every damsel who passed by and imprisoned her in their castle, so we know they were thoroughly rotten. Gawain and his companions defeat and kill them, and Gawain naturally thinks he's done a good thing. In fact, he's been pretty satisfied with his whole life so far, and certainly we're used to seeing him held up as a model of a good knight.

But then he meets a holy man who tells him that he's been a wicked and disloyal servant, and that puzzles him. The holy man won't explain why Gawain is wicked and disloyal but promises that someone else will explain it soon. And sure enough, not long after that Gawain meets a handy hermit who can explain everything—not only why Gawain was called wicked and disloyal, but also the allegorical significance of the adventure of the evil knights' castle.

> "With good reason you were called a wicked and disloyal servant. For when you were admitted into the order of chivalry you were not admitted in order that you should become a servant of the devil, but that you might serve our Creator and defend holy church and render to God the treasure which he gave you to keep, that is your soul. That is why you were made a knight, but your chivalry has been ill employed. For you have completely served the devil, and deserted your Creator, and led the most foul and wicked life that a knight ever led. So you can plainly see that he who called you a wicked and disloyal servant was well acquainted with you. And surely, if you were not such a sinner as you are, the seven brothers would not have been killed by you or with your

assistance, but they would have repented of the wicked custom they had so long maintained in the Maidens' Castle and would have been reconciled with God. Far otherwise did the good knight Galahad of whom you are now in quest: for he defeated them without taking their life. And it was not without great significance that the seven brothers had maintained this custom in the castle and detained all the maidens who came into this region, whether rightfully or not."

"Ah! sire," said my lord Gawain, "tell me the meaning of it, that I may relate it at court when I return."

"I will gladly," said the worthy man. "By the Maidens' Castle you must understand that hell is meant, and by the damsels the good souls who were detained there wrongfully before the passion of Jesus Christ. And by the seven knights you must understand is meant the seven capital sins that held sway then in the world, so that there was no righteousness. For as soon as any soul, be it of a good or a wicked man, left the body, it went straight to hell and was imprisoned there precisely as the damsels were. But when the Father in heaven saw that what he had created was doomed to such an evil fate, he sent his Son to earth to deliver the good damsels, that is, the good souls. And just as he sent his Son whom he had before the world began, so he sent Galahad, his chosen knight and servant, to release from the castle the good damsels, who are as pure and clean as the fleur-de-lys which never feels the summer's heat."

On hearing these words, he did not know what to say; and the good man continued: "Gawain, Gawain, if you would forsake this wicked life which you have lived so long, you might yet be reconciled with our Lord. For the Scripture says that not one sinner shall fail to find our Lord's mercy if he seek it earnestly. Therefore, I counsel you with my best advice to do penance for your crimes."

But he replied that he could not bear the burden of doing penance. So the hermit left him alone, without saying more, for he saw his advice would be thrown away.

The world of chivalry is turned upside down. Gawain's whole career of glorious successes has been a failure. Everything he counted as virtue is vice. The holy man even dares to tell him that he should not have killed the wicked knights, but rather made good Christians out of them! What kind of knight fights his battles that way?

Gawain's is the very sin that St. Bede, centuries earlier, had found in the British of Arthur's time. They fought the barbarians, sometimes valiantly, and who could deny that the barbarians were wicked and warlike? But never, said Bede, did the British think of preaching the gospel to them.

Gawain had fought evil knights and defeated them, but Galahad had confronted evil itself with the gospel message of forgiveness. Although Gawain tells the hermit that he can't bear the burden of penance, we might suspect that what he really can't bear is the burden of rejecting everything he believes in.

## The Proud Knight

Meanwhile Sir Hector, brother of the famous Lancelot, pursues the quest without meeting any adventure for a very long time, but at length he finds his way to the neighborhood of the castle of King Pelles. When he hears that the Grail is kept there, he rides his white stallion furiously to the castle. But when he arrives he finds all the doors shut against him.

This is not the sort of welcome a famous Round Table knight expects. So he pounds on the doors and demands entry. Who would dare bar the gates against a knight of the Round Table?

But King Pelles himself appears at the window and gives him a right royal telling off. "You shall not enter thus proudly armed while the Holy Grail is here," he declares. "For I can see that you are no knight of the quest, but rather one who serves the Fiend."

Those words infuriate Sir Hector, who redoubles his pounding and shouting. And when the king asks him who he is, he identifies himself as Lancelot's brother.

Now, when King Pelles discovers that Hector is Lancelot's brother, he's sorry he spoke so impolitely to a great and noble knight—the more so because, at that very moment, Lancelot is with him in the castle. But when Sir Hector hears that his brother is there, he turns and retreats without any objection. He remembers how a dream had warned him that his pride would keep him from the Grail. Now he understands what the dream meant. This last encounter gave him all the opportunity he needed to explore his own arrogance. He is not a worthy knight after all: he is a prideful sinner. The very accomplishments that made him a success in the world of chivalry are worthless in the quest for the Grail. For him the quest is over, and he goes back to Camelot.

+

# Chapter the Seventeenth

## The Sorrow of Lancelot; or, The Conversion of a Worldly Knight

ARTHUR'S KNIGHTS RUN HITHER AND YON in search of the Holy Grail, but most of them get nowhere. It is not the sort of adventure they're used to: they can't find the Grail just by looking in the right place or by defeating the right wicked lord.

In spite of all the running around, this quest will turn out to be an internal adventure, not an external one—an adventure of the spirit, not an adventure of the sword. Finding the Grail will depend on the state of the seeker's spirit, and Arthur's knights are slowly discovering that most of their spirits are in a sad state.

### Spiritual Lethargy

Lancelot himself comes very near to the Grail. He sees more of it than almost any of the other knights of the Round Table. But his sin holds him back. Instead of seeing the Grail clearly, he sees it in a misty, dreamlike daze as he lies exhausted on the ground near a little chapel.

When he had been there for some time, he saw coming in a litter borne by two palfreys a sick knight who was lamenting bitterly. And when he drew near Lancelot, he stopped and gazed at him, but did not say a word, thinking he was asleep. Nor did Lancelot say a word, but lay as one in a doze between a sleep and wakefulness.

And the knight in the litter who had stopped at the cross began to bewail his fate aloud, crying: "Ah! God, is there to be no end to my distress? Ah! God! when will the Holy Vessel come who will cause my agony to cease? Ah! God, did ever mortal man suffer so grievously as I suffer, and for so little guilt?" For a long time the knight thus complained and bewailed his woes and his pains to God. But Lancelot did not stir nor say a word, lying still as one in a trance, though he saw him and heard what he said.

And when the knight had waited for a long time in this way, Lancelot looked and saw approaching from the direction of the chapel the silver candelabra which he had seen in the chapel with the tapers. As he looked at the candelabra, he saw it moving toward the cross, but he could not see who was bearing it; and he was filled with wonder. Next he saw drawing near upon a silver table the Holy Vessel which he had seen once before at the Fisher King's, the very same which was called the Holy Grail.

As soon as the sick knight saw it approaching, he fell his full length upon the ground, and with hands clasped toward it, he exclaimed: "Fair sire God, who hast wrought so many miracles in this and other lands through this Holy Vessel which I see drawing near, Father, look upon me in pity, that this woe which I suffer may be speedily relieved, and that I too may enter upon the quest even as other worthy men have done." Then he dragged himself along by his arms to the stone where the table rested with the Holy Vessel upon it. And he raised himself up by his two hands until he could kiss the silver table and touch it with his eyes. As soon as he had done this he felt, as it were, cured of his woes: so he uttered a great sigh and said: "Ah! God, I am healed." And at once he fell asleep.

Now when the Vessel had stayed there awhile, the candelabra moved away toward the chapel and the Vessel with it, so that Lancelot did not know by whom it could be carried either when it approached or when it withdrew. However, it came about that either because he was wearied by his labors or because of sin which had overcome him, he did not stir when the Holy Grail passed by nor did he manifest any concern for it; wherefore later on the quest many a word of shame was said to him and many a misfortune befell him.

When the Holy Grail had left the cross and returned to the chapel, the knight of the litter rose up restored and sound and kissed the cross. At once there appeared a squire bringing some fine rich arms, and going up to the knight he asked him how it was with him.

"Well, in faith," said he, "thank God: I was healed at once as soon as the Holy Grail visited me. But I marvel at yon knight who is sound asleep and never woke up when it passed by."

"In truth," said the squire, "he is some knight who is living in some great sin which he has never confessed, and of which he is perchance so guilty before our Lord that he would not permit him to behold this fair adventure."

## The Confession

This experience leaves Lancelot filled with sorrow and close to despair. His years of glory are nothing to him. But the hermit in the chapel recognizes what's going on. Here is a gifted knight who has made poor use of his gifts. He is like the trembling servant in the parable who received a smaller sum of money from his master and hid it in the ground, while the other two more industrious servants received larger amounts and invested what they had received.

"Sire," said Lancelot, "this parable which you have shown me of the three servants who had received the besants distresses me more than anything else. For I know well that Jesus Christ furnished me in childhood with all the good graces that any man could have; but because he was so generous to me with what I have so ill repaid him, I know that I shall be judged as the wicked servant who hid his besant in the earth. For all my life I have served his enemy, and have warred against him by my sin. Thus I have slain myself in the road which one finds at the beginning to be broad and seductive: that is the beginning of sin. The devil showed me the sweetness and the honey; but he did not show me the eternal punishment to be suffered by him who travels that road."

When the worthy man heard these words, he wept and said to Lancelot: "Sire, I know that no one continues in this path you mention who is not consigned to an endless death. But just as you may see how a man sometimes loses his road when he falls asleep and returns to it when he wakes up, so it is with the sinner who is lulled asleep in mortal sin and loses the right path, but later returns to his way, that is, his Creator, and directs himself to the

High Lord who cries continually: 'I am the way, the truth, and the life.'"

At that moment he looked and beheld a cross on which the sign of the true cross was portrayed; and pointing it out to Lancelot, he said: "Sire, do you see that cross?"

"Yes," he replied.

"Then know truly," said the hermit, "that that figure has stretched out its arms as if to draw all men unto it. In like manner our Lord stretched out his arms to receive every sinner, you and all others who appeal to him, and he cries continually: 'Come, come!' And since he is so kind as to receive all men and women who return to him, know that he will not refuse you, if you offer yourself up to him in the way I describe, with true confession of mouth and repentance of heart and amendment of life. So recount your state and your affairs to him in my hearing, and I will do my best to help you to find succor, and I will counsel you as best I may."

Lancelot was still awhile as one who never admitted his relations with the queen, and would never mention them as long as he lived, unless great pressure should be brought upon him. Then he heaved a sigh from the depths of his heart and was so moved that he could not utter a word. Though he would fain speak, he did not dare, being more cowardly than brave. Meanwhile the good man exhorted him to confess his sin and have it out; otherwise he would be ashamed for not doing as he was bid, and he further assured him of eternal life if he confessed his sin and of hell if he concealed it. He spoke to him so kindly and so appealingly that finally Lancelot began to speak:

"Sire, the fact is that I am dead in sin because of my lady whom I have loved all my life, and she is Queen Guinevere, the wife of King Arthur. It is she who has given me abundance of gold and silver and the valuable gifts which I have sometimes handed on to poor knights. It is she who has set me up in great luxury in the high places I occupy. It is for love of her that I have performed the great deeds of prowess of which the whole world talks. It is she who has raised me from poverty to riches and from misery to all the blessings earth affords. But I know well that because of my sin with her our Lord is sorely displeased with me, as he clearly revealed to me last night." Then he told him how he had beheld the Holy Grail without stirring in its presence either to do it honor or to prove his devotion to our Lord.

There can hardly be a more authentic scene of repentance in the whole of literature. "More cowardly than brave," Lancelot fights the greatest battle of his life with the only enemy he has ever feared: his own sin. And that enemy is the most fearsome of all, because it is the only one that has real power over him. Lancelot leaves no ambiguity: every single thing that has ever been admirable about him—his wealth, his status, his bold deeds of chivalry—has its root in sin, not in virtue.

No wonder Lancelot had so much trouble getting that out! It would have been a hard thing to reject a love that had lasted a quarter of a century, and harder still to admit that he had betrayed his lord, whom he loved and admired.

But this confession requires more than that. It requires him to reject, unconditionally, everything he has ever prized. His great reputation is worth nothing; even all his truly heroic labors have been rooted in sin. He sees his whole world turning upside down and catches a glimpse of that kingdom where the first are last and the last first—a kingdom that has no place for his worldly success.

✝

# Chapter the Eighteenth

## In Which Sin Destroys the World, but the Repentant Sinner Is Saved

**B**ESIDES GALAHAD, THE MODEL OF THE Christian knight, there are two knights, Perceval and Bors, who trust in God to lead them where he will. Both have fallen into sin at different times, but each has the courage to beg God for forgiveness, and the earnest desire to be clean of his sins. Each recognizes that the fleeting glories of this world are nothing compared with the infinite glory of heaven.

After many adventures and tests of their wills, Perceval and Bors meet with Galahad, the good knight. The three of them are joined by nine other worthy knights from three other nations, so that the number of knights is the same as the number of apostles. Then they are privileged to be present at the feast of the Holy Grail.

## Smote Himself into the Bread

For the Holy Grail is the Eucharist itself—the Eucharist made visible, so that the hidden miracle is laid bare for good Christians to see with their own eyes. When Galahad and the rest sit down to the feast, a bishop appears from heaven and begins to say Mass over the Grail.

> And at the lifting up there came a figure in likeness of a child, and the visage was as red and as bright as any fire, and smote himself into the bread, that they all saw it that the bread was formed of fleshly man. And then the bishop put it into the Holy Vessel again, and then he did what befits a priest to do Mass. . . .
>
> Then looked they and saw a man come out of the Holy Vessel that had all the signs of the passion of Jesus Christ bleeding all openly, and said, "My knights and my servants and my true children who have come out of deathly life into the spiritual life, I will no longer cover me from you, but you shall now see a part of my secrets and of my hidden things."[1]

This is the Eucharist unveiled. The miraculous Eucharistic visions of the Middle Ages, including the paintings of the Mass of St. Gregory, give Walter Map the material for the climax of his whole cycle. And the amazing thing is that the secret wisdom of the Holy Grail, revealed to these knights who proved themselves worthy of it, is not some heretical secret knowledge kept hidden from ordinary Christians. On the contrary, it is exactly what Christians have always been taught, but now the knights have seen it with their own eyes. Blessed are those who have not seen and have yet believed.

After the feast is over, Christ sends the twelve knights to scatter through the world, as he sent his apostles before them.

## The Stragglers Return

The return from the Grail quest is a grim affair. At the beginning of the last part of Walter Map's epic, the heroes of the Round Table are sadly depleted. Most have fallen victim to their own sin. Gawain has completed his disgrace by killing eighteen good knights with his own hands in the course of the quest.

Now the atmosphere shifts from one of mysticism and wonder to one of inexorable tragedy.

Lancelot's repentance seemed marvelously sincere while he was confessing. It almost seemed cruel that he was barred from achieving the Grail. Hadn't he suffered enough?

But when he finally staggers back to Camelot, he sees Guinevere again, and we quickly discover that Lancelot can resist anything but temptation. In less than a month, he's gone back to his old ways, turning his back on the chastity that seemed like such a good idea when Guinevere wasn't around. Now we see his problem: he is still in a state of mortal sin. His repentance was superficial—it hasn't penetrated to the dark interior of his soul.

Now, in fact, he seems to be even more careless in his affair with the queen, as though he has given up the notion of covering up his sin. Soon the king discovers Lancelot and Guinevere's betrayal, and the tragedy is set in motion. The companions of the Round Table divide into factions, some going with Lancelot and some with Arthur.

Meanwhile, Arthur's bastard son Mordred seizes the opportunity to take the throne and Guinevere as well. The war against Lancelot is what gets Arthur and his best knights out of the country long enough for Mordred's treachery. Like the original sin of Adam and Eve, the adultery of Lancelot and Guinevere destroys the paradise of Arthur's kingdom. One by one the famous heroes fall. Finally Arthur returns and fights his great battle with Mordred—a battle to which Lancelot, still loyal to his old friend and new enemy, comes too late. All that is left to do is bury the bodies. Guinevere enters a nunnery; Lancelot, having lost everything he valued in the world, casts off his armor and enters a monastery, along with some of his old friends from the shattered Round Table fellowship.

## Lancelot Reaches His Goal

Lancelot now repents as vigorously as he fought every other battle of his life. He fasts, prays, watches late, and rises early—"no man alive could have suffered pain and discomfort as he did." And the result is that his quest is not the failure it seemed to be. When at last, old and worn out by vigorous penance, he knows his time is near, he asks the archbishop (who also has taken refuge in the monastery) to see that he is buried in his own home of Joyous Garde.

Then there was weeping and wringing of hands among his fellows. So at a season of the night they all went to their beds, for they all lay in one chamber. And so after midnight toward day the bishop . . . as he lay in his bed asleep . . . fell upon a great laughter. And therewith all the fellowship awoke and came to the bishop and asked him what ailed him.

"Ah, Jesu mercy," said the bishop, "why did ye awake me? I was never in all my life so merry and so well at ease!"

"Wherefore?" said Sir Bors.

"Truly," said the bishop, "here was Sir Lancelot with me with more angels than ever I saw men in one day. And I saw the angels heave up Sir Lancelot unto heaven and the gates of heaven opened toward him."

"It is but a restless dream," said Sir Bors, "for I doubt not Sir Lancelot aileth nothing but good."

"It may well be," said the bishop. "Go ye to his bed and then shall ye prove the truth."

> So when Sir Bors and his fellows came to his bed, they found him stark dead. And he lay smiling, with the sweetest savor about him that ever they felt.[2]

At last Lancelot has reached his goal. The heavenly feast, of which the Eucharist is the earthly manifestation, is his forever. "Now I know that penitence is more valuable than any other thing," says the archbishop. "I shall never leave penitence for as long as I live."

Here, after thousands of pages of manuscript, is the moral of Lancelot's story. Galahad's superior holiness enabled him to achieve the Grail when Lancelot could not. But it was not too late for Lancelot. It was not too late even when he failed in his quest and returned to his life of sin. It is never too late for the penitent sinner—not even when his sin is so great that it destroys the world.

## Heaps of Allegory

The deeper we look into the Walter Map cycle, the deeper and more elaborate the allegory becomes. Pauline Matarasso often resorts to side-by-side comparisons of passages in Walter Map and passages in Scripture. The correspondences are obvious, even though each passage from the romance, taken in its context, arises naturally from the story and doesn't look like a Scripture citation at all.

Not only the art but also the complexity of the allegorical correspondences is astonishing. Galahad enters like Christ, but also like David, whose Old Testament kingdom was a type, or foreshadowing, of Christ's kingdom. It would be easy to write a whole book about these layers of allegorical meaning, as Matarasso has done.

With such a heap of testimony in front of us, we can hardly doubt that the author of the Walter Map cycle worked hard to lay out his allegories very precisely. But we might still ask how many people in his audience understood the allegorical meanings of the story. After all, it takes us quite a bit of effort to work out the subtler shades of meaning in the romance. Could the original audience really have been that much smarter than we are?

We might be surprised at the answer. Medieval churchgoers were used to hearing allegorical interpretations of Scripture in the most ordinary sermons or homilies. Today, a preacher who makes an allegorical or a typological interpretation of an Old Testament reading has to fight for it, because allegory as a device is not used much anymore. In the Middle Ages, it was automatically assumed that almost any passage from the Old Testament hid some New Testament meaning. It was natural to think allegorically. It's quite possible that the name Galahad was enough to put people on the alert for parallels to Christ.

Still, whole layers of allegory probably escaped the original audience, too. But there again is where our author shows his genius. He left nothing to chance. The primary meaning of the story is always plain. Whenever it's necessary for us to understand the allegorical meaning of some event, a handy hermit is always nearby to explain it to us. With that minimal help, the story does its work with remarkable power: it leads us away from Ovid and toward Christ, and it does so in a way that makes us passionate lovers of virtue.

Then why all those hidden layers of meaning? What purpose do they serve?

First, the layers of meaning make the romance much richer for those who do understand them. A medieval reader would have seen the Old Testament in the same way. The story of the binding of Isaac (Genesis 22) is moving and beautiful in its literal sense, and at the end of it we learn the valuable lesson that absolute trust in God is never misplaced. We've enjoyed the story, and we've drawn from it its most important message. But the story is incomparably richer when we see the whole incident as prefiguring Christ's sacrifice on the cross. Without taking anything away from the literal story, the newly revealed allegorical correspondence adds a layer not only of meaning but of beauty as well.

In the case of the *Quest*, we might suspect that the depth of hidden allegory was also for the author's benefit. Not that adding the intricate correspondences was merely an entertaining technical exercise, like building a ship in a bottle. For Walter Map, this layering of allegory may have served a much more important purpose. We've already seen more than one writer stumble into heresy on the quest for the Holy Grail. But Walter Map's carefully developed parallels with Scripture kept him on the straight and narrow path.

## The Soul's Ascent

If Galahad were the hero of the quest for the Holy Grail, the rest of us would be hopeless cases. Galahad is the impossible standard that every Christian wants to live up to but can't. He's a sort of embodiment of the Sermon on the Mount: a model for an ethical standard that we'll never be quite good enough to meet. It's because *Lancelot* is our hero that we can have hope.

With Lancelot as his main character, Walter Map has written a "history of the soul's ascent from sin to union and oneness with God"—as Leclercq described the teaching of the great Cistercian theologian William of Saint-Thierry. Like William, Walter Map has placed the Eucharist at the center of his history. Like St. Bernard, Walter Map has a place for vigorous action in the secular world, but always with holiness as the goal in mind.

Lancelot is a sinner. Like all of us, he shares in Adam's sin; he sins so profoundly that he destroys paradise, just as Adam did. Like every sinner, he repents and slides backward into sin again.

But even when his sin has destroyed the world, it still isn't too late for Lancelot to repent. The last part of Walter Map's Lancelot-Grail Cycle has all the ingredients for a Greek tragedy, where inevitable forces leave all the characters dead on the stage and the audience staring hopelessly straight ahead. But it has one additional ingredient that turns the whole thing on its head, and that ingredient is the truth of the gospel. Because of his position as favored knight, Lancelot has more opportunity for sin than most ordinary people ever have, and his sins are of greater earthly consequence than most of our sins are. But his story ends in triumph, because the grace of God and the power of the Eucharist can overcome even the greatest of sins.

And this was the message those lords and ladies in their colorful medieval courts needed to hear. They had left Christ behind and gone chasing after a pagan ideal of love, and they had devoted their whole lives to the pursuit of what was directly contrary to Christian moral standards. Now, if the tale had done its work, they knew that what they had pursued was false and deeply unsatisfying. When they found it, they would discover that it really wasn't what they were looking for at all.

But it was not too late for them. They could still repent. Heaven—what they had really been looking for all along—was waiting to welcome them.

✝

# Chapter the Nineteenth

## In Which the Decline of Medieval Civilization Finds Its Mirror in the Decline of Romantic Allegory

*This story is as true, I undertake,*
*As is the book of Lancelot de Lake*
*That women hold in full great reverence.*

GEOFFREY CHAUCER (C. 1342–1400) was quite cosmopolitan for his time, and he wrote his *Canterbury Tales* and other works for a cosmopolitan audience. His readers and listeners in the fourteenth century were probably familiar with the best productions of the early Italian Renaissance, and they also must have been familiar with the skeptical rationalism that was just beginning to blow through Europe.

The lines you see at the beginning of the chapter are a joke.[1] The audience is expected to snicker at "The Nun's Priest's Tale" that follows, because the whole point is that it isn't true at all—no truer than the stories of Lancelot, which everyone knows are the fabrications of a more credulous age. Country people might take Arthurian legends seriously (the provincial author of *Sir Gawain and the Green Knight* wrote at about the same time as Chaucer), but educated Londoners saw them as fit only for the entertainment of the less sophisticated among them.

## The Feigned Miracle

At this time in the late Middle Ages, the medieval church had serious problems. It was wealthy and powerful, which in some ways was a measure of how seriously many wealthy and powerful people took their obligations to the church. But the wealth and the power were great temptations, and there were far too many well-placed figures in the church who couldn't resist those temptations.

Bishops sometimes became secular tyrants, ruling arbitrarily over vast territories, keeping mistresses in their palaces, and feasting while the poor starved. Profitable ecclesiastical positions were bought and sold like stocks and bonds.

Worse than all that was the appalling spectacle of disunity at the top. The Great Western Schism (1378–1417) left two or even three popes running around, each excommunicating the others and each living in pompous style.

By this time literacy was far more common than it had been before, especially among the rising middle class. When John Wycliffe translated the Bible into English in the 1380s, it allowed readers to compare the picture of the infant church in the New Testament with the current unwholesome state of the kingdom. Did Christ command that his servants should live in palaces and feast like kings? Did Paul leave a trail of illegitimate children wherever he went?

No, the would-be reformers answered: Christ commanded poverty and simplicity, and he left no doubt about where he stood on adultery. And the buying and selling of ecclesiastical offices was, Wycliffe insisted, nothing less than heresy.

Wycliffe denounced the corruption in the church (which certainly needed some denouncing) and called for Christians to live lives of simple piety. All this was good, and it could have put Wycliffe in the long line of reformers that included great figures such as St. Bernard of Clairvaux and St. Francis of Assisi.

But Wycliffe and his followers went further, attacking not only the administration but also the doctrines of the Catholic Church. They held up Scripture as the sole basis for the Christian faith, setting aside sacraments, traditions, and church leadership as unnecessary, even problematic. Most shockingly for pious Catholics, they vigorously denounced "the feigned miracle of the Sacrament" and "the feigned power of absolution."

This was a direct attack on the faith itself. It was also a direct attack on the entire basis of the best Holy Grail romances. Without the Eucharist and sacramental confession, the allegorical world of Walter Map was implausible.

Wycliffe's followers were nicknamed "Lollards"—no one knows quite where the term came from[2]—and they soon became a force to reckon with in English politics. It would be impossible for a Lollard to see the Holy Grail stories as anything but childish nonsense.

Wycliffe and the Lollards are often portrayed as the vanguard of the Protestant Reformation. Certainly many of their doctrines were similar to what later leaders of the Reformation preached. Perhaps the most characteristic of those doctrines is the notion that the Eucharist is merely symbolic, not the actual flesh and blood of Christ. This attack on the Eucharist was really the beginning of an attack on the whole traditional Christian way of seeing things. The old sense of meeting God everywhere in nature—what we might call a sacramental view of the universe—was being replaced by a new idea of nature as practically at odds with God. This new view led eventually to Puritanism, which regarded the body as a prison and the joys of nature as Satan's snares. The former, sacramental view gave us all those descriptions of spring flowers and twittering birds that begin nearly every medieval poem. It also gave us the world of Arthur. There would not be much room for Arthur in the new era.

## Led Astray by Their Longing

Wycliffe's ideas spread quickly in England. Interestingly, they ended up spreading even more in Bohemia. A number of Bohemian students had come to Oxford, where Wycliffe taught, and they took Wycliffe's ideas back with them. Those ideas later inspired Jan Hus, and then Martin Luther and the Protestants who came after him.

We can begin to see the real tragedy, and the bitter irony, of the division in the church. Many of the people who followed Wycliffe and Hus and Luther out of the church were precisely the ones who most longed to be closer to God. It was their great misfortune to be born at a time when too many of the princes of the church cared more for the things of this world than for heaven. The reformers' longing, instead of leading them into the arms of the orthodox church, led them away from a church that didn't seem to be interested.

In many ways the religious dispute was a class war. The schismatic reformers were most successful in countries where the middle classes had become most prominent. The poor might very well side with the nobility in support of their ancestral church; the middle classes, rejected by the nobles and ignored or scorned by the poor, were used to making their own way and were ready for something new.

Once the splitting started, there was no stopping it. *Sola Scriptura*—"the Bible alone"—was a rallying cry of the Reformation. But the Bible is a big book and not always easy to interpret. Even within the Catholic Church, there has always been wide latitude for individual interpretations. Once the book was taken out from under that umbrella, there were even fewer limits on where the interpretation might go.

Thus Wycliffe, following his own interpretation of the Bible, rejected the idea of the real presence in the Eucharist. Luther, a century after Wycliffe, could not give up the real presence, though he rejected the term *transubstantiation*. Most of the rest of the Reformation followed Wycliffe rather than Luther in seeing the Eucharist as a merely symbolic memorial.

So even by the 1300s, the truth of the real presence was being seriously questioned. The bread was not really the Body; the wine was not really the Blood. In their longing for a closer communion with God, the Reformers were led to reject the doctrine that the Sacrament was a face-to-face meeting with God.

Where did that leave the Holy Grail?

## Literal-Minded Romance

Arthurian allegories had never been as popular in England as they were in France. Now, in the new rational age, there was no place for allegory at all.

But Arthurian romance wasn't dead yet. There was a more literal-minded style of romance flourishing in England—one that left out Lancelot, the Holy Grail, and everything that seemed unlikely or fantastic. Returning to the apparent plausibility of Geoffrey of Monmouth, the twelfth-century chronicler of the *History of the Kings of Britain,* these new romances presented Arthur as a military hero and his knights as noble warriors.

The English were particularly fond of these pseudo-historical romances. Remember that *Sir Perceval of Wales,* a Middle English version of Chrétien's *Story of the Grail,* manages to tell the whole story without actually involving a grail of any sort. The supernatural aspects of the story have simply been tossed out, leaving us with an amusing but very down-to-earth comedy of manners.

The best of all these down-to-earth romances is the *Morte Arthure,* an epic from the fourteenth century written in late Middle English alliterative verse that presents the end of Arthur's kingdom as a Homeric tragedy.[3] There is no question of complicated religious allegory: it's a story of conflicting human motivations, betrayal and revenge, and the tragic inevitability of fate.

The epic *Morte Arthure* was fairly popular in its time. Many English-speaking readers today have never heard of it, and it's not much more than a footnote in histories of English literature. But it deserves to be remembered, if not for its own remarkable qualities, then at least because it indirectly changed the course of Arthurian literature in English. Specifically, it changed the life of one reader who went on to become one of the towering figures of English letters.

## Loyalty and Treason

If English-speaking readers know the knights of the Round Table as paragons of chivalry and virtue, it is Sir Thomas

Malory, more than anyone else, who is responsible for their reputation. So we might be a bit surprised to find that Malory, the greatest English chronicler of the Arthurian world, had a criminal record as long as your arm.

Burglary, extortion, rape, sedition—either Malory was a hardened criminal, or he had an amazing genius for accumulating false convictions. Or possibly a little of both.

Sir Thomas Malory lived at a time when civil war was England's national industry. The Wars of the Roses (1455–85) had gone on so long that they must have seemed part of the natural order. Gunpowder was beginning to make a difference in strategy, but knights in armor still fought battles on horseback. Above all, a knight was judged by his loyalty to his lord.

In a civil war, of course, loyalty to one lord is treason against another. Whatever other criminal tendencies he had, Malory had a gift for picking the wrong side. That was why he had the leisure to create such an immense work as *Le Morte Darthur:* he had picked the wrong side, and he was in prison for it.

It was not a particularly cruel imprisonment. Malory was allowed to have all the old romances he wanted to read, and he obviously had access to stacks of paper and a bottomless well of ink. He occupied his enforced leisure by compiling, translating, and adapting all the old Arthurian romances he could find, creating one gigantic book that would contain the whole history of Arthur's world. It was the first substantial prose account of Arthur in English.

The line between crime and politics blurs in a time of civil war. Nevertheless, Malory's criminal record is so extensive that we can hardly believe he was entirely innocent. So how could a vicious criminal write so convincingly about virtue?

The book itself may give us the clue. Malory's enormous *Le Morte Darthur* is not—like Walter Map's—one connected story, with plots and subplots woven together in a seamless whole. Instead of one great cohesive romance, *Le Morte Darthur* is a collection of novels linked only by a common background. And we happen to know that the first of Malory's Arthurian romances was *The Tale of King Arthur and the Emperor Lucius.* Great crashing waves of alliteration in this tale betray its origin: Malory took the story from the earlier, alliterative *Morte Arthure.* Though Malory casts the tale in prose, whole lines from the original poem are dropped, unaltered, into Malory's version.

Now, the alliterative *Morte Arthure* is the most uncompromisingly Homeric of all Arthurian romances, the one whose ethics are most purely the law of the battlefield. It is a soldier's tragedy, a tale of betrayal and revenge, and for all its literary genius it lives on a fairly low ethical plane. It must have appealed powerfully to the soldier in Malory, the knight for whom loyalty was the greatest virtue and treachery the worst sin.

But we can imagine how it might have awakened Malory's appetite for other Arthurian romances, and we can imagine him being caught up, almost unaware, into the world of Walter Map, where virtue means something entirely different. A good bit of Malory's great work is translated word-for-word from the Lancelot-Grail Cycle, and Malory must have spent quite a long time in the world of Walter Map.

Is it too much to suppose that the great allegory of Lancelot had some of its intended effect? Could Sir Thomas Malory, full-time soldier and part-time thug, have been led into a new understanding of worthiness? Could he perhaps have realized that he had been searching all this time for something more than success in battle?

Perhaps Malory himself is the greatest testimony to the power of Walter Map's narrative. For it looks as though the gripping stories in the Lancelot-Grail Cycle, and above all the romance of the Holy Grail, really did make a hardened criminal fall in love with virtue.

## Is Reason the Answer?

Still, even as Malory shows us how effective Walter Map's allegorical treatment could be, he also gives us plenty of evidence of how much the world of thought had changed.

Malory's project is very different from the Walter Map cycle. Walter Map created one great tapestry by weaving every plot and subplot into an intricate unity. Malory carefully unraveled all those strands and presented each one separately. Walter Map's work is a giant allegory; Malory's is a collection of stories.

The result of these changes is that the allegorical message fades and sometimes is hidden altogether. In Malory's section on the Holy Grail, we catch a glimpse of the allegorical world of Walter Map. But at other times it's hard to see a moral in Malory's work at all. Sometimes, indeed, we're left with the feeling that Malory himself didn't understand some of the events he narrated.

Malory is not an isolated example. The same thing was happening all over the intellectual map of Europe. The glorious mysticism of the Middle Ages was giving way to the entirely incompatible rationalism of the Renaissance. This rationalism was more than just an appreciation of the rediscovered ancient sciences. It was faith that anything could be understood—that is to say, logically proved—by any reasonably intelligent individual given the necessary information.

Oddly enough, the spirit of the new age came down to something that the medieval romancers would certainly have sympathized with: a hunger after a lost paradise, that ancient golden age when everything was good. This was the hunger fed so well by the medieval stories of Camelot.

But during the Renaissance, people considered the classical era, not Arthur's world, to be the lost golden age. Instead of Christian warriors, the heroes were pagan philosophers and rhetoricians. The ancient Greeks, and not hermit monks, were deemed the wise men, and reason and science were trusted to provide every answer society needed. The thinking was that if only the world could be run on purely rational principles, it would turn into a paradise again.

Science and reason were the answer to everything—an attitude best stated by Sir Francis Bacon, who declared that he would admit nothing as knowledge that he could not prove by experiment.

In many ways the Protestant ideas that were pushing their way across much of northern Europe were part of the same intellectual phenomenon. The Protestants who took *sola Scriptura* to its logical end refused to admit anything into their religion that could not be plainly deduced from the Bible by any literate individual. At least that was the theory, although in practice the theory often proved inadequate, as we can see from the numberless sects today based on varying interpretations of the Bible.

At first glance there might seem to be a world of difference between a Renaissance philosopher and a Puritan elder. But we can see that what Puritans and scientists shared was a kind of intellectual impatience: an unwillingness to trifle with anything that could not be thought of in concrete terms. If a thing was so deeply mystical that it could not be imagined without wrapping it in metaphors, then better not to imagine it at all. It must not be of any consequence. The world, complex though it may be, is made up of simple parts that can be understood in simple terms.

A world of pure reason had no room for tales of the Holy Grail, because it had no room for miracles. Puritans also had no room for tales of the Holy Grail, because they had no room for the miracle of the Eucharist.

## Arthur Shrinks

So where did that leave Arthur? By this time, he had come so far from his origin as a Roman-British general that he no longer seemed to have any place in the new-made rational world. Arthur stood for everything that was mystical, allegorical, and mythical in the medieval interpretation of the universe—or, as the Renaissance doubtless saw it, everything that was foggy and irrational in the benighted Dark Ages that preceded our enlightened modern world.

That probably explains why, of all the characters in Arthurian lore, the only one who kept up an active public career in the 1600s and 1700s was Tom Thumb.

> In Arthur's court Tom Thumb did live,
>     a man of mickle might,
> The best of all the Table Round,
>     and eke a doughty knight:
> His stature but an inch in height,
>     or quarter of a span;
> Then think you not this little knight
>     was prov'd a valiant man?[4]

All that was left of Arthur was a fairy-tale figure of fun. Tom Thumb was "the best of all the Table Round": metaphorically, all the great heroes of the Round Table had shrunk to less than an inch high.

✝

# Chapter the Twentieth

In Which the Long-Dormant Grail Revives
and Goes Looking for Something to Fill It

THE WORLD OF REASON AND SCIENCE did not fulfill its promise. It didn't give us the paradise we were longing for at all. In the minds of many, it created a hell on earth.

Under the rule of reason, science made enormous progress. With a better understanding of physics and mechanics, engineers created machines of all sorts—machines that did the work of ten or twenty men; machines that revolutionized how household necessities were "manufactured" (a misleading term, since it comes from Latin words meaning "made by hand").

But were the machines our servants or our rulers?

## The Age of Ugliness

The whole industrial age that began in the 1700s in England was irredeemably ugly to sensitive souls. Horrid black soot hung in the air; linens put out to dry came in gray after a few hours, and ancient landmarks and new constructions alike turned a uniform black. Centuries of tradition in crafts were forgotten as the giant smoke-belching factories learned to manufacture all the necessities and luxuries that once had been made by hand. Worst of all was the mind-sapping regimentation of life, with a huge working population condemned to spend their whole lives toiling all their waking hours in the hot, grubby, deafening, and often deadly factories—all to support families imprisoned in identical houses in hot, grubby, deafening, and often deadly cities, where disease, crime, and vice festered unchecked.

If the picture we paint seems relentlessly grim, it's because we've painted the industrial age the way it looked to the artists and poets who rebelled against it. Once again, we find the best thinkers of the age longing for a lost paradise. They compared the modern age with a fancied medieval past where the world was clean and colorful and art was true and honest. And what they saw through the distorting lens of nostalgia was what they tried to recreate in the present. They did not succeed in derailing the industrial age, of course. But they did succeed in creating permanent beauty, and that is about the most that can be said for any artist.

If science, the child of the Renaissance, was making the world a horror, then the cure for it might be found before the Renaissance. The medieval styles in all the arts, dismissed as "Gothic" or barbarian by those of

Renaissance tastes, might be just what the industrial world needed. Suddenly the Middle Ages looked like a lost paradise.

With surprising speed, all the arts turned medieval. Gothic architecture was revived so successfully that it dominated church building for another century. Poets wrote roundelays and triolets in their best imitation of medieval style. Musicians began tentatively groping among forgotten medieval manuscripts for "Gothic" music. Painters imitated the flat perspective and formal expression of the medieval miniatures. All the latest styles were six hundred years old.

## Camelot Revived

With all the arts reaching back to the Middle Ages for inspiration, it was only to be expected that Arthur and the Holy Grail would come back into favor. Nothing was more colorfully medieval than the world of Camelot. What might have been a little surprising, however, was just how spectacularly popular the world of Arthur turned out to be. And we can attribute much of that popularity to Tennyson.

After Malory, Alfred, Lord Tennyson, is the greatest name in English Arthurian literature. His *Idylls of the King*, published in 1859, brought Arthur to the masses again and formed what has ever since been the popular notion of Camelot and the Round Table.

Tennyson's characters live in Malory's world. His poems are based on Malory's tales—which explains why, like Malory, he gives us not a unified epic but a series of discrete though related stories.

What Tennyson adds is a careful exploration of the characters' inner lives. Malory's characters come to vivid life mostly in what they do. Tennyson's characters paint subtle self-portraits in introspective soliloquies. One of the best monologues is Lancelot's report to Arthur after the end of the Grail quest:

> O King, my friend, if friend of thine I be,
> Happier are they that welter in their sin,
> Swine in the mud, that cannot see for slime,
> Slime of the ditch; but in me lived a sin
> So strange, of such a kind, that all of pure,
> Noble, and knightly in me twined and clung
> Round that one sin, until the wholesome flower
> And poisonous grew together, each as each,
> Not to be pluck'd asunder.

Tennyson seems to have hit Lancelot's character exactly right here. Unfortunately, the Grail quest itself is a bit of a disappointment in Tennyson. As the official poet of Queen Victoria's England, he had to remember that he stood for the things England stood for, Anglican Christianity among them. And, during that time at least, Anglicans set themselves apart from Roman Catholics, and they did not believe in transubstantiation. For a long time, if you wanted a government job in England, you had to swear an oath that you didn't believe in transubstantiation. Many a secret Papist with a conscience was outed by that simple test.

But what is the Holy Grail without the miracle of the Eucharist? If the Eucharist is not miraculous, then the Grail is not much more than a collector's item—a valuable antique to be coveted, but not the fulfillment of our deepest longing.

Still, if Tennyson—like Malory before him—seems to have diluted the allegory, he did at least bring Arthur and his knights to the attention of the greater reading public through poetry of real power and beauty. And it was the Holy Grail that seemed to fascinate the reading public most. Not since the High Middle Ages had there been such an explosion of interest in the Grail. For a people who longed for a lost age of beauty, the Holy Grail seemed to contain within it everything that was beautiful.

But where the medieval writers had given us all sorts of Grails, from broad platters to magic rocks, the nineteenth-century artists and writers who took up the Grail had reached a nearly universal agreement: the Grail was the Holy Chalice, the cup of the Last Supper. The agreement was so universal that Richard Wagner, when he made an opera out of Wolfram von Eschenbach's *Parzival,* changed the gem in Wolfram's story to a chalice. A gem just didn't seem right. Even for Wagner, whose religious opinions could hardly be described as orthodox Christian, the Grail was a Eucharistic image.

## Faith in the Eucharist Revived

If medievalism had been limited to the arts, we might dismiss it as but one fashion in the endless parade of fads that have swept through the art world without leaving a permanent mark on the minds of the public at large. But it was more than an artistic fad. Medieval art and thought had been rejected as dry and primitive for hundreds of years; now the well of science was coming up dry, still failing to satisfy our longing for something greater. A return to the medieval mind-set promised a way out of that failure—starting with the acknowledgment that there really was something greater than the material world, something that couldn't be proved by experiment but had to be reached by faith.

So even as the architects were rediscovering the Gothic and the poets were rediscovering the roundelay, medievalism was taking hold in religion, too—with surprising results for the intellectual life of Anglican Britain.

In 1833, the first of a long series of pamphlets called *Tracts for the Times* came before the public of England. These little tracts, written by an Anglican named John Henry Newman and his close friends, created more of a sensation than their authors had expected.

One of Newman's closest friends was a young man named Richard Hurrell Froude, who had gone medieval in religion the way the rest of Europe had gone medieval in the arts. "He had a deep devotion to the real presence in which he had a firm faith," Newman remembered later. "He was powerfully drawn to the medieval church, but not to the primitive."

Like artists and poets of the time, Froude longed for a lost golden age—an age when faith was pure and powerful, and above all an age when the sacrament of the Eucharist was understood for the miracle it was.

Newman absorbed his young friend's enthusiasm for the medieval in religion, although he remained "most firmly convinced that the pope was the Antichrist predicted by Daniel, St. Paul, and St. John." In other words, Newman imagined an Anglican Church rebuilt on the model of the medieval church yet relieved of the burdensome allegiance to Rome. In fact, Newman and Froude saw themselves as pioneers of a second reformation, and Newman in particular took Luther as his model.

For ten years, Newman preached in his tracts a "middle way" between popery and Protestantism: an Anglican Church built on Tradition, apostolic succession, and a high conception of the Eucharist. He saw the Anglican Church as "but the local presence and the organ" of the one, holy, Catholic, and apostolic church, dependent on the ancient Tradition of that church as much as the other local presences in other countries were, indeed as much as Rome itself was. It could be a church in which the Eucharist was truly celebrated, in which Christ was really present to his people.

For some who read the tracts and heard his sermons, Newman's ideas were a revelation. The Anglican Church had always been deliberately broad-minded, which in practice meant that it was a bit fuzzy on what it actually believed. Tradition was not much preached, except the already ancient tradition of the Reformation—which was mainly seen as a rebellion against the authority of the pope rather than as any positive development in doctrine.

Now it seemed as though the ancient traditions of the church could be reclaimed for the Church of England. There was a chance that the color and fervor of medieval religion could come back to save England from its dull industrial regimentation. The Eucharist, truly and properly understood as Christ's real body and blood, might bring about that longed-for reprieve from the grayness of modern life. The *Tracts for the Times* were being snatched up as fast as the presses could print them.

On the other hand, Newman's critics reacted with outrage and even horror. It looked to them as though Newman was simply letting popery in through the back door. It was whispered that there might even be some sort of conspiracy involved, and that one day good Anglicans might wake up to find the pope's storm troopers banging down their doors.

It turned out that the critics knew Newman better than he knew himself. There was no conspiracy, no new armada to invade England and grind it under the heel of the Vatican. But Newman's ideas were leading him closer and closer to Rome. In 1845, just as the controversy—and even panic—over those ideas was reaching its peak,

Newman astonished England by entering the Roman Catholic Church.

Newman had found his Holy Grail, his closer communion with God in God's kingdom on earth. Thousands went with him in the years to come. Hundreds of thousands more have followed him since then, led into the Church of Rome by Newman's elegant and persuasive writings.

The strange irony is that the church he abandoned was deeply marked by his ideas. The Anglican Church today is more broad-minded than ever, but its renewed emphasis on traditional liturgy and the apostolic succession bears the unmistakable marks of Newman and his friends. By the time he entered the Roman Catholic Church—where he rose to become a cardinal—Newman had already made a permanent mark on the church he left behind.

## The Pre-Raphaelite Grail

Meanwhile, back in the art world, the longing for a golden age of Eucharistic faith and the embrace of everything medieval were leading painters and illustrators in the nineteenth century to the Holy Grail. The artists known as the Pre-Raphaelites showed an especially keen interest in the Holy Grail. The Pre-Raphaelites were medievalists who rejected the academic trends in art and went back to what they thought of as a purer, sincerer time—the time before Raphael.

Some of the very best of the Holy Grail pictures come from this group, from Dante Gabriel Rossetti, Edward Burne-Jones, and others who were fascinated by the subject and went back to it again and again. Tennyson might have felt compelled to tone down the symbolism of the Grail, but the Pre-Raphaelites and their followers felt no such constraints.

Perhaps their deep immersion in medieval art had given them more sympathy with medieval ideas. Or perhaps the deliberately medieval style of their pictures gave them what moderns call "plausible deniability": they could always take refuge in the claim that they were merely trying to evoke the true medieval spirit. In any case, their Grail scenes are uncompromisingly religious, and therefore uncompromisingly Eucharistic.

Like Froude and Newman, these Victorians were stumbling onto the truth: the Eucharist was what they were really longing for after all. That was the antidote to the mechanical ugliness and spirit-sapping regimentation of the industrial age.

It should not surprise us, then, that the growing awareness of the presence of Christ on the altar was reflected in a growing awareness of the presence of Christ in the poor and forgotten—the people left behind by the Industrial Revolution—and, even worse, the people caught in the machinery. Multitudes of well-known charities date their foundation to this fertile era. Even the misguided attempts to study the poor as though they were some curious phenomenon were usually motivated by genuine feelings of charity, however strange and even amusing the results might have been. Once again, a Eucharistic culture was rising.

But at the same time, other ideas were making themselves heard. Was religion really the route to paradise? Or could it be replaced by a secular philosophy that would build a paradise on earth?

## When the World Went Mad

A thousand years from now, historians may look back at the twentieth century as the age when the world went mad. Or perhaps they'll look back and call it the age of broken dreams.

It was an age when ancient wisdom was rejected just because it was old, and when serious attempts were made to govern society by reason alone. Four of those serious attempts left us names that will live on in history: Hitler, Stalin, Mao, and Pol Pot. Each one of them lived by a dogmatic faith that a paradise on earth could be created if the unreason and superstition of the past were abandoned and reason and logic were given free rein.

Fascism collapsed in the middle of the century, and communism collapsed at the end of it. Communism replaced fascism in much of Europe; then capitalism replaced communism in most of the world. Still, the Communist societies that replaced the Fascist dictatorships, and the capitalist societies that replaced the Communist dictatorships, were no better than their predecessors at providing a paradise on earth, although the capitalists were perhaps a bit less efficient at creating an earthly hell.

In spite of the mad swings from one form of government to another, or perhaps because of them, it was also an age of great saints. For every Adolf Hitler, there was a Maximilian Kolbe, who died a martyr in a concentration camp, giving his life in exchange for another prisoner's. And if there is one lesson to be learned from the madness of the twentieth century, it is that the saints always win in the end.

In Hitler's concentration camps, St. Maximilian Kolbe modeled the crucifixion of Christ and shared in Christ's resurrection. Hitler preached a thousand-year empire based on the latest race theories; Stalin and Mao preached the inevitable victory of communism based on the proofs of Karl Marx. The thousand-year Nazi empire lasted about a decade; communism could not survive the twentieth century. Yet the Christian Church is still here in the twenty-first, still preaching Christ crucified, a stumbling block to the Fascists and foolishness to the Communists.

## The Constant Danger

It would be far too easy to dismiss people like Pol Pot and Hitler as purely evil, which is a very comfortable way of dealing with them. Evil seems to explain everything, but in fact it explains nothing. Pol Pot did not make a solemn league with Satan in his university days; he did not consciously decide that he would choose the evil over the good and align himself once and for all with the dark side. Evil isn't like that. Evil always disguises itself as good, and we can be sure that the eviler Pol Pot became, the more convinced he was that he was the best of men.

There was something that he wanted with such passion that he moved by easy and almost imperceptible steps from murder to war to genocide on a scale almost impossible for us to comprehend.

And the horrible truth is that, at a deep, human level, the thing he wanted was precisely the same thing all of us want. We want to get back to paradise. We want to walk with God in an uncorrupted Eden. And our desperate longing can lead us to desperate crimes.

✝

# Chapter the Twenty-First

## The Longing Fulfilled; or, The End of the Quest

H ERE WE ARE, VERY NEAR THE end of our quest, and we have a little time to rest and look back at where we've been. The story of the Holy Grail—that is, the story of the story—has taken some surprising turns, but one thing has been consistent all the way through.

From start to finish, just one idea has driven our quest. We feel instinctively that we had paradise and lost it; we ache with all our being to get it back. We want to walk with God again.

The early Christians, from the apostles on, knew that they had found what they were looking for in the Eucharist, in which God the Son comes to us in the bread and wine. "We cannot live without the Mass," they told their persecutors—and they would die rather than give it up.

But they knew that the cup of blessing could also be a cup of judgment. "For all who eat and drink without discerning the body, eat and drink judgment against themselves," St. Paul had warned them—and they took the warning seriously.

## Distractions along the Way

The stories of Arthur are also all about that longing for paradise lost. The Welsh who told those stories were descendants of Arthur's people. They knew they had once ruled the pleasantest kingdom in the world, but God had taken it away from them because of their sins. And right at the beginning of that story, when Arthur was still a bright and living memory, St. Gildas the Wise already had the answer to their longing: repent!

That's what it really takes to get back to paradise. The lost world is ours again when we're reconciled with God.

Still, we don't always recognize the longing for what it is. When Christians grow too complacent, when we forget what a miracle every Mass is, then we can be tempted by other things that look like more direct routes to the fulfillment of our desires. Our profound longing can lead us into the profoundest sins.

That's exactly what happened when medieval high society went mad for love. Human love is the greatest of created goods; it really is a glimpse into the divine life, the perpetual and unchanging love of the Holy Trinity. But we fall into all sorts of sins when we make it the end of our quest rather than a signpost along the way. The strikingly religious language used by the romancers of the school of courtly love shows that this cult of love was more than a distraction: it was a substitute for the true religion.

Nevertheless, some of the disciples of love couldn't help seeing that their god was a false god, and that human love was not really the answer. The greatest of all the poets of courtly love, Chrétien de Troyes, was also the first to see beyond the prejudices of the courtly lovers, and to begin to suspect that the unfulfilled longing was something spiritual—something to do with our relationship with God.

## The Great Allegory

Chrétien began a tantalizing story in which an ignorant young hero who has "forgotten God"—as we might say Chrétien's own audience had done—sets out on a quest for a mysterious grail that carries a single Mass wafer to an ailing king. But Chrétien never finished the story.

Left unfinished, the tale drew in other writers who were entranced by its allegorical possibilities. Pulling in elements from wildly diverse sources—old Celtic adventure tales, apocryphal legends of Joseph of Arimathea—they began to construct a whole allegorical universe revolving around the Eucharist. The grail, object of all desire, became the Holy Grail, and its contents the blood of Christ; it was the cup of the Last Supper, in which Joseph of Arimathea had caught Christ's blood at the foot of the cross.

All this feverish interest in the Grail came just at a time when the medieval church was wondering how to win back its flock, many of whom—even among the nobility, and sometimes even among the clergy—were ignorant of the most basic Christian principles. It occurred to a few religious minds that the popular romance might be used to bring the disciples of love back into the orthodox church, and that the story of the Holy Grail was just the thing to do it.

Led by that ambition, "Walter Map"—who may have been one person or several—constructed the greatest of all allegorical romances: a gigantic, sweeping epic with Lancelot as its hero and the Holy Grail, the cup of blessing and the cup of judgment, at its center. It is an amazingly rich, satisfying, and orthodox allegory of the soul's ascent from sin to salvation. Everything in the romance has a meaning beyond itself, and everything leads us not only to see the truth of Christian doctrine, but also to long for that close communion with God that the Holy Grail represents.

Because Lancelot is the hero in the Walter Map cycle, he's also the model for us. And it's because Lancelot is our model that we can have hope. Galahad achieves the Grail, but Galahad is too perfect for us to emulate. Lancelot is all of us, with our multitude of sins and our inflated self-image that needs to be punctured.

Like us, Lancelot is subject to the sins of this world, but he sees clearly the emptiness of the good things achieved by sin in comparison with the infinitely greater good of communion with God.

His longing leads him to something that looks like repentance, but in Lancelot's backsliding we see the difference between true and false repentance. We also see the course of most Christian lives. We all go through these repeated cycles of sin and repentance. We all think we can take just a little bit of the old world of sin and death with us on the road to life.

But in the end, Lancelot does achieve the Grail—after his sin has destroyed his world. It still isn't too late for him. He achieves the Grail in heaven. Angels welcome the repentant sinner, the prodigal son, to the heavenly feast.

## Ups and Downs of Eucharistic Culture

Walter Map's romance was a profound expression of what we could call a Eucharistic culture—a culture that was keenly aware of the real presence of Christ's body and blood on the altar, and therefore just as keenly aware of Christ's body in Christ's members. It was an age when hospitals and orphanages were founded, an age when the ideal of Christians working together to make the lot of their fellow creatures better was sometimes, for fleeting moments, made a reality.

But intellectual fashions change as fast as any other fashions. The rationalistic (which is rather different from rational) world of the Renaissance had no room for mystical allegories, because in fact it had no room for mysticism at all. Reverence for the Eucharist declined, and many Protestant groups abandoned faith in the real presence altogether. There was no market for allegorical romances about the Eucharist.

And loss of faith in the real presence of Christ on the altar was mirrored by a loss of faith in the real presence of Christ in Christ's members. The industrialization of European society turned people into machines, valued only for what they could produce.

It was probably that horrifying regimentation of humanity that set the stage for the revived interest in things medieval, including medieval romances, medieval art, and—most important—medieval religion.

The twentieth century seemed to think it could do without religion, but here in the twenty-first century we find that the rationalist fads of the twentieth century are extinct or dying, and religion is stronger than ever. Now we're looking back once again toward that lost paradise. And the Good News is that we can find it again.

## Finding the Holy Grail

For the Holy Grail is not far off—not in heaven or beyond the sea, but as close as our parish church. When we have made ourselves ready to receive the holy, *God comes to us.*

That's what the Grail seekers discovered in the old stories. No amount of seeking, no matter how diligent, would find the Grail for them—unless the Grail was ready to be found. They might gallop across a continent and never catch a glimpse of it, but it was ready for them when they were ready for it.

Being ready for it is the real quest, and a lifelong adventure. Worthiness is what we're really looking for, as Lancelot discovered. He could see the Grail, but he could not approach it while in a state of mortal sin. The cup of blessing is also a cup of judgment, just as St. Paul told us—not because God is a God of rage and revenge, but because holiness and sin just don't mix. God's judgment and God's mercy are the same thing: both expressions of God's eternal love for people. *Psalm 85*

This is why *confession* plays such an important part in the Walter Map romances. The most dramatic moment in the whole cycle is not a thrilling battle or a haunting mystery: it is the moment when Lancelot confesses that everything in his life, everything that he thought he loved, everything that made him glorious in the eyes of the world, is sin.

And it *is* a thrilling battle, and it *is* a haunting mystery. To defeat a well-armed foe was routine for Lancelot, but here he must defeat evil itself, the evil that has sunk its roots into everything he does. And then comes the haunting mystery of God's forgiveness, the sacrament by which God wipes away the sins of the unworthy and makes us worthy in spite of ourselves.

This is why confession and repentance are inexpressible blessings. The Holy Grail—face-to-face communion with God—is our prize, and it is the only thing that can satisfy that infinitely deep longing that every one of us feels.

Gawain's rash oath was *right*. It was worth giving up everything—even Camelot, the Round Table, and the kingdom of Britain—to pursue the Holy Grail. It was rash only in the sense that no one is truly prepared to give up the things they love the most. Yet real repentance means turning away from everything that holds us back.

But the reward, like our longing, is infinite—infinite life, infinite joy, infinity itself. This is what that spiritual code is really driving us to seek. Heaven comes down to earth in the Eucharist, and the heavenly feast is ours. Let us all confess our sins, repent, and praise God for making us worthy to receive his Son.

# AFTERWORD

## THE ANTIDOTE TO GRAIL NONSENSE

THE FIRST THING WE NEED TO remember about the legend of the Holy Grail is that it's a *story*. Not "just a story"—any more than the parable of the prodigal son is "just a story"—but a story and not a history. The best of the medieval romances were written not to record a true account of actual events, but to teach the truth about the Eucharist—just as Jesus told the parable of the prodigal son not to record an event in Near Eastern past, but to teach the truth about God's love and forgiveness.

Seeing the legend as a story and not as a history is the antidote to all the nonsense that passes for Grail literature in today's bookstores. Almost all the erroneous books about the Holy Grail begin with one erroneous premise: that the tales of the Grail were meant to convey historical truth rather than moral truth.

There are a number of strange Grail theories advanced in modern literature. We might divide Grail writings today into two basic categories, according to what they try to tell us the Grail is.

In the first category are the Grail romances that document, in a veiled way, the existence of the actual cup of the Last Supper somewhere in Europe. These writings sometimes contain holes in plot and reason, but they are often the product of sincere piety, or at least antiquarian interest, which usually makes them harmless enough.

In the second category are romances whose writers suggest that the Grail is a metaphor for some closely guarded secret, kept over the centuries by some incredibly efficient conspiracy. In these writings the Grail represents pagan goddess worship or a sacred bloodline—or a combination of the two.

## A Nazi Obsession

*Indiana Jones and the Last Crusade* was fiction, of course, but at least one thing about it was true: the Nazis really were obsessed with the Holy Grail. To Hitler it was a symbol of blood—not the blood of Christ, but pure Aryan blood, the holiest thing in the neo-pagan Nazi religion. The sacred Aryan bloodline had been defiled by race mixing and needed to be purified; that was what Hitler thought the medieval romances (especially Wolfram von Eschenbach's *Parzival*) were really about.

Hitler had his beliefs about the Grail, but to Heinrich Himmler, the head of the SS and a notoriously gullible occultist, the Grail was a real object with magical powers, and he spent quite a bit of money funding his pet archaeologist's expeditions to find the Grail among the ruins of the Albigenses' last stronghold.

In the version of the legend that Himmler subscribed to, the Cathari, the "pure ones" who were at the top of the Albigensian hierarchy, were supposed to have been the guardians of the Grail. When the Albigensian Crusade closed in on them and it was apparent that all would soon be lost, they hid the Grail somewhere in the vast warrens of caves surrounding their mountain fortress of Montségur.

Himmler was nuts for Grail lore and the Arthurian legends in general. At the SS headquarters in the castle of Wewelsburg, Himmler recreated the Round Table, with seats for himself and a dozen of his most trusted officers. There was a place for the Grail, too, when it was found. But the pet archaeologist failed to come through. Curiously, not long after he gave up and left the SS, the archaeologist fell off the side of a mountain.

The Nazis are history: they're still horrifying to think about, but they're gone. A surprising number of their ideas, however, are still floating around in one form or another. Some of Hitler's and Himmler's oddest ideas about the Grail have slipped into popular culture and show every sign of sticking there.[1]

## A Holy Bloodline

In 1982, a hodgepodge of pseudo-history and anti-establishment ranting called *Holy Blood, Holy Grail* hit the best-seller lists, and it's been a standard item in book-shops ever since. The idea behind the book, to summarize briefly, is that the Holy Grail legends actually refer to a sacred bloodline. So far this is Hitler's interpretation. But the exciting new twist is that this royal bloodline is a deep, dark secret. The royal family turns out to be none other than the offspring of Jesus Christ and Mary Magdalene.

According to the book, the secret knowledge that they had children has been suppressed by the established church for two millennia but kept alive by a conspiracy (involving the Cathari) through all that time until today, when the world apparently is ready to be trusted with the secret again.

Why did the church suppress the knowledge so thoroughly that it lay undiscovered for two thousand years, until some hack writers with a hunch blew the whole thing wide open? Because, the authors say, the church, rebelling against the original intention of Christ himself, needed to reinforce patriarchal authority. Thus it was imperative that all knowledge of women's roles in the early church be deleted from accepted history. Mary Magdalene represents the lost appreciation for the "sacred feminine" that Jesus and his first followers expressed but that the antifeminist Catholic Church could not allow.

This secret knowledge of the truth about Christian origins is often attributed to the Gnostics, a group of heretical sects that blossomed in the first few centuries of the Christian era.

The Gnostics are convenient pegs upon which to hang alternative Christian history. There were so many Gnostic sects, and they believed so many wildly different and contradictory things, that it's easy to say "the Gnostics" believed practically anything we want to believe they believed. The one thing they all had in common was the thing that made them "Gnostics": their claim to possess a secret knowledge hidden from the hoi polloi.

"Gnostic" comes from the Greek word *gnosis,* which comes from the same root as our word *know.* The idea of secret knowledge that is available only to the initiated, coupled with the idea that *you* can be one of the initiated, is powerfully attractive, as any advertising writer can tell you. Even when the secret knowledge turns out to be nonsensical, or at least incomprehensible, it's still our big, important secret, and that's enough to make it seem worth keeping. It helps if the secret knowledge is expressed in arcane jargon so that no one is quite sure what the big secret is, because no one, after putting so much effort into becoming one of the chosen few, will dare say, "I don't get it" to one of the other insiders. Gnosticism had all these things going for it, especially the arcane jargon.

All the things that made Gnosticism so popular in its own day still work today. *Holy Blood, Holy Grail* and the many imitators that have followed it promise to let us in on a gigantic secret that has been kept from us for centuries. Who can resist a promise like that?

## A Surprise Best Seller
Just when it seemed that the "holy blood" idea could be safely ignored on the back shelves of bookshops, along

came another surprise best seller to turn the fad into a mania. *The Da Vinci Code* probably owed some of its early success to author Dan Brown's skill at constructing an entertaining by-the-numbers thriller. He gives us all the right ingredients, with an edge-of-your-seat cliff-hanger at the end of every chapter to keep us reading right to the end. The plot is a bit unbelievable, but so is the plot of the average secret-agent movie; we accept it because we know it is entertainment, not a documentary of true events.

What really cemented the book's place on the best-seller lists, though, is the author's insistence that the more far-fetched elements of his plot—centuries-old conspiracies, including the one postulated in *Holy Blood, Holy Grail*—are absolutely true. "FACT," the book states at the beginning: "All descriptions of artwork, architecture, documents, and secret rituals in this novel are accurate." We could easily take that as just another novelist's trick to add verisimilitude to his tale—if the author weren't just as insistent outside the book. Some reviewers took him at his word: "His research is impeccable," said the *New York Daily News,* which ought to know impeccable research when it sees it.

But most of that research was done in books that come from what we have a right to call the wacky fringe. Many of the ideas Brown puts forth as fact are either unlikely or impossible. For example, Brown took from *Holy Blood, Holy Grail* the idea that Jesus was not seen as divine or as "Son of God" until the reign of Constantine.

A glance at the New Testament is all it takes to prove otherwise: "You are the Messiah, the Son of the living God" (Matthew 16:16); "In the beginning was the Word, and the Word was with God, and the Word was God. . . . And the Word became flesh and lived among us" (John 1:1, 14); "For God so loved the world that he gave his only Son" (John 3:16); "in the presence of God and of Christ Jesus, who is to judge the living and the dead" (2 Timothy 4:1); "through the righteousness of our God and Savior Jesus Christ" (2 Peter 1:1); "I, Jesus, who sent my angel" (Revelation 22:16); and on and on. No respectable scholar, and in fact hardly any disreputable scholars, would suggest that these books were written after the time of Constantine, or that the passages that refer to Jesus in unmistakably divine terms were late interpolations. Yet to discover these passages, all we did was open the New Testament and flip to a few familiar verses—which is not very elaborate research. Ignoring this evidence takes a lot of willpower.[2]

## Why All the Nonsense?

These strange conspiracy theories reject what for the medieval authors was the central point of the Holy Grail story: the real presence of Christ in the Eucharist. That was the secret of the Grail for Walter Map. Perhaps many of us cannot bear the idea of meeting Christ face-to-face; if he is in fact divine, then would he not have the authority to stand in judgment of us? It's much safer to demote Jesus to an ordinary human, even if we have to postulate a conspiracy lasting two millennia.

But if we reject the central theme of the Grail stories, then why do we continue to consume so much Grail nonsense? Why is the Grail still such a powerful idea, even when we've contemptuously poured out its contents?

Perhaps the Grail still represents that unfulfilled longing for the divine that all of us feel, even when we refuse to be led to the only thing that could possibly fulfill it. Once we have rejected Christ and the Eucharist, all that's left for us to do is make up new grails—unholy ones—that represent the things we wish we could find at the end of our quest. Since our sin blinds us to the greatest possible good, we substitute all kinds of lesser goods—love, sex, secret knowledge, money. The object of all desire is right there in front of us, but we scurry past it as we chase after petty treasures.

This is why we see so much silliness about the Grail in books, movies, and television documentaries. Once we pour out the blood of Christ, the Grail is just an empty cup, and we can fill it with anything we like. Who's to say we're wrong? So we make the Grail represent the "sacred feminine," or some secret alchemical wisdom, or a breathtaking historical mystery, or just about anything else we care to make it represent. We want the Grail romances to be true, but on our terms.

The real miracle of the Grail romances is that they *are* true—not historically, but morally and spiritually.

They show us the world as it really is, with blessing for the worthy and judgment for the unworthy. They show us how to make the miraculous leap from unworthiness to worthiness. They show us how to meet God face-to-face.

And that's what we really want. All the other things we think we want are snares—decoys that keep us from pursuing the real object of all desire. It's right there in front of us, on every altar in Christendom. Are we worthy to achieve the Grail? Are we ready to be satisfied? Are we ready to walk with God in paradise?

# NOTES

## Chapter 3

1. From the ancient acts of the North African martyrs, cited in Andre Hamman, *The Mass: Ancient Liturgies and Patristic Texts* (Staten Island, NY: Alba House, 1967), 16.

2. Garrett Pierse, *The Mass in the Infant Church* (Dublin: M.H. Gill, 1909), 119.

3. Mike Aquilina, *The Mass of the Early Christians* (Huntington, IN: Our Sunday Visitor, 2001).

4. This is exactly what has happened to one of the most famous claimants to the title of Holy Grail: a chalice in Valencia that consists of an ancient and very plain drinking cup set in an elaborately ornamented stand. There is good evidence to show that this cup was *believed* to be the cup of the Last Supper at least as early as the 500s.

## Chapter 5

1. Gildas the Wise, *On the Ruin of Britain,* 24; trans. J. A. Giles.

2. Great Britain is so called to distinguish it from lesser Britain, or Brittany.

3. The Annals are written in Latin. Some scholars believe that the word *shoulders* is a misinterpretation of an original Welsh word for "shield," the two words being nearly identical in early Welsh.

4. Gildas, *Ruin of Britain,* 26.

5. Bede the Venerable, *Ecclesiastical History of the English Nation,* trans. J. Stevens (London: J. M. Dent, 1910), chap. 22.

## Chapter 6

1. Lady Charlotte E. Guest, trans., *The Mabinogion* (Mineola, NY: Dover, 1997).

2. Caitlin Matthews and John Matthews, *British and Irish Mythology: An Encyclopedia of Myth and Legend* (London: Diamond Books, 1995).

## Chapter 7

1. The coronation drew astonished expressions of outrage from Constantinople. Didn't the pope know that the world already *had* an emperor?

2. These Eucharistic miracles are carefully analyzed and categorized in Miri Rubin, *Corpus Christi: The Eucharist in Late Medieval Culture* (Cambridge: Cambridge University Press, 1991).

3. The sociologist Rodney Stark has piled up an impressive amount of evidence to show that "the masses knew next to nothing in terms of basic Christian culture" ("Secularization, R.I.P.," *Sociology of Religion* [Fall 1999]). Yet we have, on the other hand, innumerable instances of laypeople who felt the irresistible call of Christ and acted on it: St. Francis of Assisi is one of the best-known examples. Perhaps the medieval world was a good bit more like ours than we usually think.

4. Stark, "Secularization, R.I.P."

5. Dom Jean Leclercq and others, eds., *A History of Christian Spirituality,* vol. 2, *The Spirituality of the Middle Ages* (London: Burnes & Oates, 1968).

## Chapter 8

1. *Guigemar,* lines 19–21; new translation.

2. Translated by W. W. Comfort, and so throughout. Walter Map [attrib.]. *The Quest of the Holy Grail,* trans. W. W. Comfort (London: J. M. Dent and Sons, 1926).

3. Comfort, W. W., trans. *Lancelot, or, Knight of the Cart.*

4. The German romance of *Lanzelet,* by Ulrich von Zatzikhoven, though it was probably written shortly after Chrétien's *Knight of the Cart,* refers often to a now-lost source. Possibly the original Lancelot story was a Breton abduction-and-rescue adventure, and Chrétien's novel contribution—or more likely Marie's, since he says the treatment was hers—was making Lancelot Guinevere's lover. That would explain the shock value of revealing the name so late: Chrétien's audience knew Lancelot, but the idea that he was the queen's lover was a big surprise to them.

## Chapter 9

1. Note, in particular, that it is not a cup or chalice.

2. It wasn't the first time Chrétien had abandoned a promising story. *Knight of the Cart* was completed by someone else, apparently with Chrétien's approval.

## Chapter 10

1. Pauline Matarasso, *The Redemption of Chivalry* (Geneva: Droz, 1979), 11.

# Chapter 11

1. Richard Barber, *The Holy Grail: Imagination and Belief* (Cambridge, MA: Harvard University Press, 2004), 42.

2. The prose romance had been invented before, in classical times, and a few of these romances survive, but the medieval prose romance seems to be an independent invention.

3. Wolfram claims to have had a source for his book: he attributes the tale to a certain Master Kyot, who taught himself Arabic so that he might learn the true story of the Grail from secret Arabic documents. The story is so fantastic that it seems most likely to be one of Wolfram's little jokes.

# Chapter 12

1. Étienne Gilson, "La Mystique de la grâce dans La Queste del Saint Graal," *Romania* 51, (1925); our translation.

# Chapter 13

1. P. M. Matarasso, trans., introduction to *The Quest of the Holy Grail* (London: Penguin, 1969), 13.

## Chapter 14

1. Comfort, *Holy Grail*. And so throughout.

## Chapter 16

1. Richard Barber, *The Holy Grail: Imagination and Belief* (Cambridge, MA: Harvard University Press, 2004), 4.

2. Ibid.

## Chapter 18

1. Sir Thomas Malory, *Works of Malory,* ed. Eugene Vinaver (Oxford: Oxford University Press, 1971). In this section, Malory translated Walter Map almost word for word into his own characteristically vigorous English; we have modernized the language.

2. Ibid.

## Chapter 19

1. "The Nun's Priest's Tale," in *Poetical Works,* ed. F. N. Robinson (Boston: Houghton Mifflin, 1933) lines 4401–3.

2. Perhaps from *loll,* because they lolled about lazily; or from a word meaning "mumbling," because they sang hymns softly to themselves; or—as their opponents

explained it—from the Latin word for "weeds," because they sprang up like weeds among the good crops.

3. Scholars call it the *Alliterative Morte Arthure,* to distinguish it from a stanzaic *Morte Arthure* written at about the same time.

4. From an anonymous poem printed in 1630: *Tom Thumbe, His Life and Death: Wherein is declared many Maruailous Acts of Manhood, full of wonder, and strange merriments: Which little Knight liued in King Arthurs time, and famous in the Court of Great Brittaine.* Spelling and punctuation modernized.

## Afterword

1. To be fair, the Nazis did not invent the idea of the Grail's association with the Cathari; they merely adopted and amplified a strong local tradition around Montségur. But it may be true that Hitler was the inventor of the interpretation that sees the Grail as a sacred bloodline rather than a tangible object.

2. Two very good books debunk the historical claims of *The Da Vinci Code.* Carl E. Olson and Sandra Miesel have painstakingly analyzed and refuted the pseudo-hisoty in the novel in *The Da Vinci Hoax* (San Francisco: Ignatius Press, 2004), giving us scholarship that should satisfy the most rigorous academic. A more

populr overview of the arguments comes from Amy Welborn in *De-Coding Da Vinci: The Facts Behind the Fiction of the Da Vinci Code* (Huntington, IN: Our Sunday Visitor, 2004).

# SELECTED BIBLIOGRAPHY

Barber, Richard. *The Holy Grail: Imagination and Belief.* Cambridge, MA: Harvard University Press, 2004.

Bede the Venerable. *Ecclesiastical History of the English Nation.* Translated by J. Stevens. London: J. M. Dent, 1910.

Cable, James, trans. *The Death of King Arthur.* London: Penguin, 1971.

Chaucer, Geoffrey. *Poetical Works.* Edited by F. N. Robinson. Boston: Houghton Mifflin, 1933.

Geoffrey of Monmouth. *The History of the Kings of Britain.* Translated by Lewis Thorpe. London: Penguin, 1966.

Gilson, Etienne. "La Mystique de la Grâce dans la Queste del Saint Graal." *Romania* LI (1925).

Guest, Lady Charlotte E., trans. *The Mabinogion.* Mineola, NY: Dover, 1997.

Lacy, Norris J., ed. *The Arthurian Encyclopedia.* New York: Peter Bedrick Books, 1987.

Leclercq, Jean, François Vandenbroucke, Louis Bouyer, and Louis Cognet, eds. *A History of Christian*

*Spirituality.* Vol. 2, *The Spirituality of the Middle Ages.* London: Burnes & Oates, 1968.

Loomis, Roger Sherman, and Laura Hibbard Loomis, eds. *Medieval Romances.* New York: Random House, 1957.

Malory, Sir Thomas. *Works of Malory.* 2nd ed. Edited by Eugene Vinaver. Oxford: Oxford University Press, 1971.

Marie de France. *The Lais of Marie de France.* Translated by Glyn S. Burgess and Keith Busby. London: Penguin, 1986.

Matarasso, Pauline. *The Redemption of Chivalry.* Geneva: Droz, 1979.

Matarasso, P. M., trans. *The Quest of the Holy Grail.* London: Penguin, 1969.

Mills, Maldwyn, ed. *Ywain and Gawain; Sir Percyvell of Gales; The Anturs of Arther.* London: J. M. Dent, 1992.

Rubin, Miri. *Corpus Christi: The Eucharist in Late Medieval Culture.* Cambridge: Cambridge University Press, 1991.

Stark, Rodney. "Secularization, R.I.P." *Sociology of Religion* (Fall 1999).

Tennyson, Alfred Lord. *The Works of Alfred Lord Tennyson.* New York: Grosset & Dunlap, 1907.

Wace and Layamon. *The Life of King Arthur.* Translated by Judith Weiss and Rosamund Allen. London: J. M. Dent, 1997.

# A Special Invitation

Loyola Press invites you to become one of our Loyola Press Advisors! Join our unique online community of people willing to share with us their thoughts and ideas about Catholic life and faith. By sharing your perspective, you will help us improve our books and serve the greater Catholic community.

From time to time, registered advisors are invited to participate in online surveys and discussion groups. Most surveys will take less than ten minutes to complete. Loyola Press will recognize your time and efforts with gift certificates and prizes. Your personal information will be held in strict confidence. Your participation will be for research purposes only, and at no time will we try to sell you anything.

Please consider this opportunity to help Loyola Press improve our products and better serve you and the Catholic community. To learn more or to join, visit **www.SpiritedTalk.org** and register today.

—THE LOYOLA PRESS ADVISORY TEAM